TWO WORLDS AS ONE

by

VAL WILLIAMS

Published by:
Red Wing Publishing
1 Brecon Road
Blackburn
BB1 3JY
United Kingdom

First Edition 2001

ISBN   0-9540-179-0-0

CONTENTS

INTRODUCTION

COMMUNICATION IS LOVE

Those higher minds from the Spirit world show amazing trust in the mediums to whom they give information, and I will always be grateful that they have communicated, knowing absolutely that I would give the message exactly as it was given to me, without adding to it, or leaving anything out. All too often we become aware that mediums do not give their messages exactly as received, something which always saddens me, for the real content of the message becomes lost in the translating sometimes. We must always remember we are not the messages, merely the messengers!!

Such instances of trust, communication etc, have meant such a lot to me that, from time to time, I have kept notes in order that I can always refer to the various dossiers of evidence I have been privileged to be a part of, whether from the standpoint of giving the messages or receiving them. Therefore, everything you will read can be verified and proven — this is not a book of fiction, but a factual account of the way the Spirit world interacts with us and our world — it is a wonderful two way form of communication and we are so much a part of it, if we would only extend our senses beyond the physical.

That is the challenge the Spirit world have offered to us, and I hope that something in this book will encourage you to seek your own individual truth, as well as encouraging you to look back to truths that may already have been shown, but which you have just taken for granted.

I cannot prove to you that there is life after death, but I, and mediums like me, can provide evidence that communication is coming from a seemingly unknown source. After all, if a total stranger can give you intimate details relating to the life of a loved one who is now in the Spirit world, and if that communicator offers information, through the medium, of present day events, where do you think it comes from?

The medium makes the offering and you take the information and prove it for yourself, and hopefully for others around you who may be interested.

What, many people ask, is the point of communication? Does it disturb the dead? Aren't mediums just psychic gravediggers?

These are just a few of the questions we are asked, on a regular basis, by those who doubt and those who fear the truth.

The point of communication is to allow those in the Spirit world to speak their truth.

It cannot disturb the dead, for there are no dead — merely personalities who have survived physical death, and whose souls have travelled on.

Mediums cannot disturb the so-called dead, for they have no power — mediums are simply like a telephone exchange, waiting for the right time to be called, and then putting people in touch with each other.

Until I began writing this book I had not realised just quite how passionately I felt about my work for the Spirit world, and I know now how defensive I sometimes am, for I know that those people who communicate are your relatives and friends, as well as my relatives and friends, and I am always honoured when asked to pass on a message of love, or of hope, or of comfort, and it saddens me when those who do not understand condemn mediums without any proof whatsoever of the negativity they accuse us of.

In this wonderful country of ours, we work within the confines of the law — we are accepted because we have proven ourselves to be honest, and yet we must always accept that there will be those who feel threatened by us.

I wish you well with your personal search, and can only encourage you to seek, ask, and ask again until you are satisfied with the answers you are offered in response to the questions you have, regarding mediums and mediumship. But, remember, mediums only have the knowledge afforded to them in the light of their own experience. If you always remember this you will not be disappointed in any individual, but will continue to search until you establish your own truth.

COMMON SENSE

As I begin, I am wondering why I'm writing this book, and who would be interested in it, and then I remember that, many times during the past 18 years I was told by various mediums that I would write a book, and so, having met people who have put their thoughts onto paper to benefit those who wish to read what they have written, I can only do what I feel is right, at this particular time. Have you ever noticed how sometimes we try very hard, and yet that which we wish to do the most does not happen?

And have you further noticed those times when, without even seeming to try at all, the things we need to have happen for us, actually do?

The lesson seems to be that there IS a Divine law working for us, that power of love we call God and sometimes, when we just give in gracefully instead of trying to work the system for ourselves, all is truly well in our world.

Are you the same person you were 20 years ago? Do you wish that you were 20 years younger and yet with the same knowledge you have now? Knowledge is something we don't always recognise, and yet something which replaces doubt, belief systems, curiosity, but without doubt, and therefore testing, without having received a belief system from somewhere, and without curiosity, how would we gain knowledge?

It is only, on reflection, that I can see clearly the pathway that was so obviously mapped out for me, though I don't exactly know from where or when, and quite frankly I don't question absolutely everything anymore, having received enough proof that Universal law is truly working in my life, and that I just need to get out of my own way sometimes.

Do you often wonder about the seeming coincidences that occur in your life, and have you noticed how often those circumstances brought about through the seeming coincidence, absolutely help or add something to your life? If this is something you have not yet thought about, maybe something you will read in this book will give you reason to question, reason to be curious about some of the circumstances of your life, and who knows, like me you may eventually establish, for yourself, knowledge that there is a guiding force working its way throughout your life, a loving power that protects you, offering you so many opportunities you have previously not even thought about.

Instead of going off at a tangent, which I frequently seem to do, I will try to begin at the beginning of my search for my own knowledge, and I hope some of my experiences will arouse within you a reason to examine your life again, particularly those of you who, having suffered, can see no purpose to your suffering.

It would be easy for me to say that there is no such thing as suffering, that everything is Karmic law, and therefore, something we have to experience, but as a medium, and a Spiritualist, if I am to work within the framework of the law of this land, then I must be able to prove what I say. Everything I shall say has been witnessed, and can be proven, for not to be able to do so, would not encourage you to establish your own dossier of real evidence, which then transforms your belief system to real knowledge.

Mediums are often accused of being airy-fairy, of using imagination and not common sense — nobody can tell you that a medium is honest, and proving truth to you — only you can do that for yourself, so do be willing to keep a reasonably open mind, always remembering that God actually gave us seven senses, the seventh being common sense, and if you will always use this approach in your search for truth, you cannot go wrong.

FOREWORD

THE TURNING POINT

Many times throughout our lives there are turning points, which when we look back are quite major events, although at the time they did not seem to be so.

During my time investigating spiritual truths, and spiritual guidance, which has now spanned almost 20 years, I have come to have absolute respect for the 'hand that guides us'. With this has also come a sure knowledge that we are all loved, guided and protected throughout our lives.

Where I feel confusion arises is when people feel they are more special than others and when they view traumas as punishments. Sometimes I feel the only way to cope with sadness, anger and confusion is to acknowledge there is no punishment from an unseen source, as some would have us believe, but rather constant opportunities to learn, through experience, and through learning to grow and evolve.

Does that sound a little deep?

It only appears to be too deep when you are focussing on your own needs and problems — when you can detach from your emotional sadness, or negativity, and view your situation dispassionately you will understand what I mean. Having had so many years of sadness, lack of confidence, doubt and confusion, I was so surprised when I became consciously aware of my spirit communicator, or 'my voice' as I call him.

Later you will see many references to him and on one occasion I refer to him as 'the voice of my soul' — please don't misunderstand — this is NOT my inner voice manifesting through my thoughts, and therefore some part of my imagination — this is an actual voice, which I hear, and which resounds throughout my being — a voice which speaks with such truth, such conviction that I must always listen.

I first heard this particular male voice in 1967, the year before I married. I was visiting my future sister-in-law, and a group of people were discussing a difficult situation with a young lady. They were planning to do something about it and were making their plans there and then. During this time 'my voice' told me who the culprit was, my immediate reaction being that I was wrong and my imagination was playing tricks on me — had I listened the next 20 years would have been very different. However I did not listen, so married my now ex-husband and there began a period of 20 years, which was certainly one major turning point and one I bitterly regret.

How many times have you not followed a hunch, an inner voice, or sound advice and how have you regretted it? Imagine then having a very real voice, albeit one you do not know, speaking inside your head and offering advice — strange? Of course! Something to make you think? Absolutely!

If there were times that that particular voice spoke to me during the next 15 years I ignored it, becoming more and more unaware of my contact with the Spirit world, due to the many negative aspects of my marriage.

OPENING CHAPTER

THE QUEST BEGINS

I can feel, within my very being, that my life is going to change beyond recognition, and even as I write the words I know I am beginning to accept that. I am suddenly reminded of a time, just over 21 years ago when, sitting in my grandmother's mobile home in Cornwall, I was told by a gypsy that I would write a book one day.

At that time I was married, very unhappily, as my then husband was an incredibly insecure person, who allowed me no personal freedom whatsoever. I was not allowed to have a job, except in mother's shop, nor was I allowed to venture out on my own, except during the day when I was taking care of our son.

Imagine my reaction to be told that one day I would write a book, and that I would travel the world etc, etc. I just assumed the woman to be totally mad — after all, at that time I knew nothing about psychics — my grandmother had merely seen this woman's advertisement in a local newspaper, in which she had advertised herself as a clairvoyant and healer, and actually grandmother felt she needed some healing to her back. She, therefore, booked the woman to come to her home, and told me I would have a private reading with her, something I knew nothing at all about.

At that stage I had only ever been to a lady who was known to all the locals in my area of Lancashire as Daisy Denby — a truly remarkable woman, but nevertheless someone I visited more for a laugh than anything else. Usually one person booked for a few of us to go to see her, and the last time I had been was around the age of 16 years. Now here I was at the age of 29 once again being given information by such a person, not understanding any of it.

I wonder now, if having been given the idea, it has rested in my subconscious mind ever since, until the time was exactly right. You see, during the past 18 years, during which time I have worked actively as a medium, I have been offered many opportunities for more publicity, have been asked by two people if they could write a book about me and my life. I was also approached, on four separate occasions, by TV producers or directors who wished me to make "shows" for them, but on each occasion it did not feel right, and so I rejected it.

Not until the middle of last year did the pieces of this particular jigsaw begin to fall into place. I have such a love of my work with Spirit, and of the communicators who choose to give me their trust in passing on messages to their loved ones, that I would only ever consider working with people who understand that, and who would promote my work with love, and the integrity that I have offered to the Spirit world.

Last year I met such a person, someone who has, for a similar number of years to myself, been investigating the truths that the Spirit world offers to us, and when we have held discussions during which we have tried to understand why we met we both realise that it was simply part of a long-term plan formulated by higher minds from the Spirit world in order that we can work together to offer the readers of this book an opportunity to analyse its contents and search for the truth within.

It is now almost 20 years since I first began investigating the truths offered to us by the Spirit world, despite having voices in my head, visions and a "knowing" ever since I can remember. Unfortunately, I did not know who to ask about my happenings and so, for most of my childhood, I felt I was wicked and that I would probably end my days in a mental home. It therefore seemed easier not to talk to people about the things I knew, or sensed, or saw. Looking back to those tortured times makes me feel very sad, wondering how much I actually missed, and yet accepting that, at that time, it was not necessary for me to know of the Spirit world and the great truths that could be offered to us, or to know of the guidance that is for ever at hand, when we truly need it.

I will ever be grateful to the lady who pushed me in the direction of a spiritualist church, a lady who advertised herself as a Famous Sussex Coast Clairvoyant, who my friend Muriel and I went to see one Friday afternoon in 1980.

Thanks to her direction I began a search that began in 1980 and which will continue until I draw my last breath, but what a joyous search it has been — and the truth I have found that is the most astounding is that I have found MYSELF!

How many of you reading this feel lost and alone, and how many of you when seeking the help and guidance of a medium feel that the medium cannot possibly truly understand how you feel, because mediums have not experienced personal trauma? They are just told everything by Spirit aren't they?

What a misconception!!!

Mediums of quality, able to transmit messages of comfort and truth from your loved ones in the Spirit world, are able to do so because they have had personal experiences of sadness, trauma, anguish and loss which have led them to investigate human emotions, the need for establishing that there really is a Spirit world, and that our loved ones can and do survive death — a good medium FEELS your sadness and pain, I can assure you, for from the point of understanding the medium has been trained to know what you need, and can transmit correctly the feelings and thoughts of your loved ones.

Ask yourself now — have you ever had a reading or public message from someone purporting to be a medium which left you feeling totally unaware that the Spirit world were communicating, even though some of the information may have been correct?

Have you, on the other hand, ever received a communication, after which you felt warm, loved, content to know that there truly is a Spirit world, and that communication is a reality?

Now compare those feelings, and you will KNOW whether or not you have had a message delivered by a medium who has genuinely received communication from one of your loved ones — from someone who truly cared for and about you.

During the past 19 years I have received so very many messages from so very many mediums, and, in fact, from 1980 until 1987 I kept each and every one. I still have them now, and can use them as references always.

One message which truly does stand out was from Don Galloway, who I first saw in 1982 at Blackpool Spiritualist Church. I had just begun to sit in a private circle, at the home of a lady called Margaret, and she suggested I may like to go to the Blackpool church as there were to be four mediums doing a demonstration. I was very excited because all the mediums were "international mediums", and one of them was Don Galloway, who I had not heard of at that time, having only recently begun to investigate mediumship through the churches.

Margaret always liked to sit on the front row, and so, of course, I sat with her. During the evening Mr Galloway (as I then thought of him) said he wanted to speak to someone at the front of the church with the name of Williams. I literally froze, reminded of the time I had won at bingo and I was too scared to call out.

Margaret put my hand up, and immediately Mr Galloway said to me "Now, dear, for nine years you have been looking for an anchor, and you have found it in Spiritualism and you damned well won't let anyone take it from you, will you?". "No" I bleated, feeling absolutely petrified — Don then went on to give me a wonderfully evidential message from the Spirit world, and I left the church later feeling I was floating on cloud nine — although desperately unhappy, and very restricted in life. No-one knew except my friend Muriel, and she couldn't possibly have given this medium all the information he gave to me, so how did he know so much about me?

That was the real start of my investigating proper mediumship, and it has been, and will continue to be a life-long task, sometimes wearying, mostly fantastically joyous, especially since my own mediumship developed very quickly.

SPEAKING OUT FOR SPIRIT

In a small way I was able to repay the favour, in a manner of speaking, when a year or so later I once again attended a demonstration given by Don Galloway at Blackpool Church.

Muriel and I arrived to find a very quickly filling church, and so we sat about half way back on the left hand side. During the course of the evening I was once again given a message by Don, and when he sat down I saw the most astounding light surrounding him which prompted me to ask my "voice" what this was, but instead of an answer I was given a communication for Don.

Well, of course, there was no way I, who had only just begun developing my spiritual gifts, could possibly be expected to give someone like Don Galloway, international medium, a message from the Spirit world — who did I think I was?

However, I did tell Muriel about the message, and that I did not intend to give it to him, I was surprised when she said "If we are given something for someone else we have to give it — we cannot just keep it". I, therefore, made a "bargain" with Spirit, by saying that if everyone else left the church, and Don was the only person remaining, I would give him the message, and if not I would not. To be honest, I felt I was on pretty safe ground, because when demonstrations were ended, the mediums always went down the stairs from the stage instead of coming into the main body of the church.

To my surprise, as the church started to empty, I saw him come into the church instead of going down the back stairs with the other mediums, apparently coming to speak to someone. During the next ten minutes the church emptied, until only Muriel, myself and Don were left, at which time Muriel said "Well, go on then, give him his message". I truly wished the floor would open up and swallow me whole but of course it did not, and I stammered out the information very quickly, giving the name and relationship of the communicator, and offering him the message, which I did not understand at all at that stage, but which I have since come to know was absolute encouragement from Spirit for Don to establish the Lynwood Fellowship, a charitable organisation, of which Don is the founder and chairman, and for which I have been greatly privileged to work on many occasions.

During the early stages of our investigations into mediumship Muriel and I would save with great difficulty in order to spend time with like-minded people searching for Spiritual truths. Sadly on many occasions we did not find a welcoming or loving atmosphere, often feeling that the seminars were more like clubs rather than organised events – in other words little cliques of people who did not wish to include newcomers.

FRIENDS

MEETING MURIEL

My search actually began in 1980, although at the time I certainly didn't realise it, but I need to go back a little bit further to give a little background to the story.

I was married in 1968, and during that same year gave birth to David. Life was very difficult emotionally, and financially, and to help make ends meet I would knit hats for my mother's wool shop, this not always allowing me enough of that precious commodity, quality time to spend with David, something I have often regretted, but I believe, as parents, we can only do our best at the time.

By the age of seven David, being a particularly intelligent boy, was bored, bored, bored. A workmate of his father, together with his girlfriend, was a volunteer at the Fleetwood Sea Cadet Base, taking classes of seven to ten year old boys, teaching them the basics of navigation, marching etc. It seemed that this could be a good thing for David to do, and he was very keen to join, and so we enquired. The reply was quite surprising — "We are full but I am fed up of going up there twice a week, and if you are willing to take on these classes your son can join". It seemed absolutely ridiculous, as I knew nothing about teaching, nothing about navigation, marching or anything else associated with the Sea Cadets.

However, David was so keen to join I finally agreed, and duly presented myself at the Sea Cadet Base, and the fun began. Each night prior to a cadet night I would read a bit of the phonetic alphabet, or a bit about basic navigation, and then teach it the following night, and little by little I realised I was actually enjoying it, encouraging the boys to feel confident. I marched those boys up and down Fleetwood Promenade as if I actually knew what I was doing, and eventually I think I did.

Little did I realise how important this time was, in terms of giving me confidence to deal with the general public, confidence to know that I could encourage the natural abilities of people (many of the little boys were very shy, but I would encourage them to find what THEY were good at as individuals, would hold concerts etc, and deal with them in very positive ways — something it has become natural to do within my classes, encouraging people to develop their natural mediumistic gifts, here and abroad).

For those of you who are shy, as I was at that time, there is something quite wonderful about serving customers in a shop with a counter between you and them — you are not quite as vulnerable as when, for instance, you stand on an open stage. For this reason many mediums, when first starting, feel more comfortable working in places where there is an enclosed area in which they may stand, but with confidence gained through encouragement it becomes easier to leave behind that comfort and walk forward, knowing that Spirit will help you.

Looking back those years at the sea cadets were the opening in life that I needed, because I was married to an obsessively jealous man, had no social life until going to the sea cadets, nor was I "allowed" to work outside the home until my son was four, when my mother needed someone to run one of her shops, and so from selling wool, haberdashery and children's clothes in a tiny shop on Lord Street, Fleetwood, I progressed to teaching little boys, to going to Spiritualist churches and daring to stand on a Spiritualist church platform and give messages from the Spirit world — what a transition, and how I have thanked those workers in the world of Spirit every day of my life since that time.

MY FRIEND MURIEL

At this stage, I suppose it is only fair to offer you a little understanding of who Muriel is.

I understand you have a need to know, because at every seminar and during every lecture, at some time I find myself saying "And I said to my friend Muriel...", or "When Muriel and I were...", and then I relate particular instances of when Muriel and I were together and the things we learnt and discussed.

It has become quite comical because now, wherever I go, people ask if Muriel is real.

Oh yes, I can assure you she is very real, and I hope you will meet her one day.

It was because of Muriel that I first went to the Spiritualist Church, although our meeting was in a very different place — the Fleetwood Sea Cadet Base. In 1977 we formed a friendship, and often during the week she would leave her nursing job and come to meet me at the shop I was running, part time, for my mother. We would then go to the same cafe for lunch, and then while the afternoon away around Fleetwood.

We actually became very firm friends, doing everything together, always going to Sea Cadet events together, and eventually going to the Spiritualist Church together. Sadly, our feelings about Spirit, and the workings of the Spirit world, were so very different that once we began developing our understanding and our gifts we could not understand each other, and so we drifted apart, merely acknowledging each other's presence when met at the various churches in the area.

It was some three or four years later that, one day, having had some very bad experiences in so-called development circles, I asked if she would like to come to sit in circle with a few of us who were sitting at my home. She did, but the circle broke up, so Muriel and I decided that once a week we would sit simply to meditate.

At that stage neither of us knew exactly where our Spiritual gifts were to take us, but Muriel was doing healing and I was giving a great deal of accurate clairvoyance, yet neither of us could find time to meditate, and so we agreed that every Friday evening, for one hour, we would sit at my house. (My then husband and son were fully occupied at the Sea Cadet Base and so the evening was available to us — I had given up my duties there to concentrate on my developing mediumship).

This we did for 12 months, never missing an evening unless it was absolutely impossible for us to meet, and oh did we love that time with the Spirit world. During the year Muriel and I both became aware of the incredible closeness of the Spirit world, and the Spirit people, and yet it was not until some time later that we realised how much true knowledge was being fed to us subconsciously — knowledge that we have both been prepared to share with others ever since, Muriel as an excellent circle leader, and me in my capacity as a teaching medium, which is something I love doing.

It was Muriel who would come with me to each new church or venue, Muriel who saw how nervous and frightened I was of letting Spirit down, Muriel who put up with the tears and tantrums, and Muriel who always told me I could do better than I was doing.

Our friendship has survived our divorces, many personal upsets, many tragedies, and we are now entering our 24th year of friendship — a friendship that has truly stood the test of time — to this day we rarely agree on much, BUT when it comes to matters of the Spirit our ideas and ideals match exactly, for our only concerns are for TRUTH, TRUTH, TRUTH, and nothing else matters.

In our search for truth we have laughed together, cried together, shared our thoughts jointly and individually with anyone who needed a little help, or a push in the right direction, and I thank God every day that she came into my life.

I can only hope that anyone reading this who is hoping to develop their own gifts of mediumship will have a Muriel to fall back on, because you will need that, I can assure you. The path of mediumship, whilst rewarding in so many ways, is not an easy one, but you must keep at it, for only when you do can you be true to yourself and who and what you are, and need to be.

So now you know who Muriel is, you will understand why I refer to her so many times, and so I need make no excuses for including her so often.

LOTTE

Having introduced you to Muriel, I think it only sensible at this stage to talk to you about another person who had a major influence on my life — my friend Lise-Lotte James, who passed to Spirit at Christmas 1997, mainly because there are many references to her throughout the book.

Lotte was, undoubtedly, a special person for she was very much her own person, and in many ways she taught me to dare to be my own person, instead of someone who was always anxious to please everyone else.

We met, many years ago, when I was working for the Lynwood Fellowship. I was asked by someone accompanying Lotte if I would be willing to travel to Portsmouth to do workshops and services, etc, for the Portsmouth Temple.

I said I would and some time later it was arranged. Lotte offered to do the hosting, which meant my staying with her and her husband Ernie at their bungalow in Horndean, Hampshire. Little did I realise, at that stage, how intertwined our lives would become, how much we would help and support each other, or how suddenly she would pass to Spirit — so, although I am still deeply saddened by the loss of someone very special in my life, I am eternally grateful that we were brought together in the first place.

WE'LL SHOW YOU

PROOF OF SPIRIT

There have been so many instances when the Spirit world have chosen to let me know they are guiding me, but none have been so dramatic as in those early years.

During 1992 I was particularly unhappy and was asking more and more for proof that there really was a Spirit world, and that the Spirit people would look after me, and help me to understand life and what it was about. It seemed to others that my mediumship was unfolding very quickly, but on a personal level I was finding it more and more difficult to cope with the circumstances surrounding my so-called marriage.

Having sent out thoughts for more proof, yet not specifying in which way that proof should come, I found I was totally unprepared for it when it came.

There were two particular instances which left me in no doubt at all, and I would like to share them with you.

The first occasion was on a day when I was very sad, so I decided to look for a ring which had been given as a gift and which had made me very happy. Nowhere was it to be found — I searched every inch of the house, in every drawer and cupboard, even looking through pillow cases and pillows, to no avail. Suddenly my voice said "Look in Alan's tool box", my first reaction was that now I knew I was kidding myself when I thought there was a voice guiding me.

However, always the intrepid explorer when it came to proving Spirit, I went into the garage where he had a toolbox, the type that opens out and has several compartments. I opened it and thanked God that nobody was watching me search in there for a missing ring!

Just as I decided to give up the search I caught sight of an old fashioned tin containing something called "Imps" — tiny liquorice sweets — which apparently help the throat. What a peculiar thing, I thought, and felt the urge to open it. Inside was the most beautiful mother-of-pearl cross about 1" long with silver decoration. I removed it from the box and took it upstairs, and for a long time sat just looking at it, somehow knowing it was special and meant for me.

For some days I said nothing, then one day I asked Alan if I could have something from his tool box. He looked at me oddly, then said "If you want to" — no doubt wondering what on earth I wanted nuts, bolts or screws for.

When I showed him the cross he denied all knowledge of it, and so I knew it was a gift, to me, from the Spirit world, and twice afterwards I received information substantiating my belief that it was, indeed, an apport.

Many people seem to believe that an apport is something that "just appears" — but years of experience have taught me that a physical article, presented by Spirit as an apport, is merely a physical object which has been de-materialised from one place, and re-materialised at its destination.

That cross became an integral part of my work for Spirit. I held on to it tightly during every service and demonstration, until one day I was going to do a demonstration and could not find it anywhere. I became quite upset, believing that if I did not have it with me, I could not do the demonstration.

Another lesson learnt, because of course I did do the demonstration, and with just as much confidence and accuracy as I would have done had I still been holding the cross.

When I was given evidence of the fact that the cross was a gift from Spirit I was further told, on each occasion, that it was actually a gift from the nun who was guiding me at that time — a gentle soul who never pushed me, but rather taught me that, under her guidance, I could learn how to communicate messages of comfort, in a loving way, to those seeking the truths of Spirit return.

THE CROSS I WEAR

Now I wear a cross, and some people ask me why. The first symbol I ever saw when I made contact with the lovely nun was a gold cross with light coming from its centre. One day, while shopping in Fleetwood at the end of February, so quite near to my birthday, I was passing a greengrocer's shop which was on the corner of Poulton Road. I was amazed to note that there, in one of the windows, was a display of jewellery. The sun was shining and I was just admiring the jewellery when suddenly I saw a stream of light coming from one of the trays. It so reminded me of the cross shown to me by the nun, with the light coming from it.

I rushed to Muriel's and told her all about it. She, too, had seen it and also wanted it badly, but when I explained the Spiritual significance of it and she agreed I should have it. It was therefore bought as a birthday gift for the sum of £19 — an incredible amount of money at the time it seemed — and I have worn it every day since, never feeling quite right without it.

There were many instances of proof of the presence of this nun, including a psychic drawing of her, which I will talk about later.

THE PROPELLING PENCIL

Another example of an apport was just as obvious — every time I was given a message by another medium I was told to sit down with pen and paper and do inspirational writing, something I knew nothing about, and when I did consider it I always thought other people could do a better job, so I didn't bother. The messages about this were coming in thick and fast, every time I went to a Spiritualist church, but still I did not "get the message" so to speak.

One day at home, having just cleaned the whole house, I went into the bedroom for something, and there on the floor by the bed I noticed a yellow propelling pencil. Thinking "How strange, no one uses such a thing today", I immediately took it downstairs and asked my son and then husband whether they knew where it had come from, and as usual, I received blank stares which made it obvious they thought I was being a little "strange" again.

My next visit to church confirmed that the pencil had, indeed, been brought by Spirit operators, to jog my memory regarding the writing I had been told, many times, I should do. This time I got the message, and from that time, giving a little time each day, I began a series of communications from the Spirit world, some prose, some poetry, examples of which are contained within two small booklets I have produced.

Whilst I have other examples of the very positive and physical ways Spirit proved to me their presence in my life, and the good and loving ways they were willing to work with me, to avoid confusion I don't wish to offer too much at this stage.

Each time I had absolute proof of my helpers, each time I had real evidence, I was given time for the information to sink in for me to analyse the whys and wherefores — and each time more proof was being planned, which I was then given WHEN THE TIME WAS RIGHT.

Time is a precious commodity to those of us who live in this material world, but something which matters little to the Spirit world and its operators and communicators.

They, not we, know when we are ready to receive information, guidance, advice, and so we must simply put out the thoughts for the help we think we need and let them do the rest, knowing they will not let us down.

MY VOICE

In 1981 I first began to understand my gifts properly. I began to receive messages from the Spirit world — I saw the Spirit people quite clearly, and sensed them as well. However, I used to hear other mediums say things like "My Chinese guide is telling me or my Indian chief is telling me" and I began to feel quite worried about this, as no-one seemed to tell me anything. I simply had thoughts in my head which I knew were messages for people, and sometimes I saw the Spirit communicators, and whilst most people said the messages were very accurate I did not have any of these High Guides that everyone seemed to know they had.

I took a deep breath one night and asked a male medium, who had just taken a service, how I would know who was guiding me. His response being "Who do you see before you give a message?" I said "No-one." "Well, what do you hear?" I said "Nothing, I just have a lot of thoughts". "Well" he said, leaving me thinking that I obviously must be making it all up, as I did not have one of these guides.

As usual when confused I went home, sat up in bed, and began a conversation with whoever was willing to listen from the Spirit world, just hoping that someone cared enough to listen to my ramblings. This time I told "them" that I was obviously committing some terrible sin by saying these things without knowing who was telling them to me, despite their being correct, and that perhaps I should stop immediately before I caused someone some great harm.

In times of doubt of this nature I always received the answer very quickly and from some other medium, and this time was no exception. Very soon I was being told time and time again that although we have guides it is not necessary to know the name or status of the person, but rather to come to know the personality and nature of the individuals who guide us, for then we know where we are placing our trust.

I then did as I always do to this very day — I left it in the hands of Spirit to give me the information and I did not have to wait very long.

A medium called Mary Duffy was due to come to Blackpool church, and I thought it would be nice to have a sitting with her, so I booked it and waited for the day to arrive. During the sitting she described an Indian (North American) to me, saying his name was Red Wing, and that he was my guide — I took it all with a pinch of salt because, of course, this cannot be proven, OR CAN IT? It would be ten years before the knowledge of Red Wing and his presence in my life was to be fully established, but I now know him very well.

During the next ten years little by little the jigsaw pieces were given to me. Various mediums made constant reference to this particular Native of America, complete with description, many saying he had the nose of a Greek, which seemed rather strange.

Two mediums from Fleetwood Church actually said they saw him transfiguring (I am sure they saw this clairvoyantly) through me, and they each described exactly the same man.

One day, almost ten years later, I had some friends visiting and so Muriel and I decided we would go into Blackpool for a girls' day out, shopping. They all wanted to go to a second-hand book shop, which I found incredibly boring, and so I stood outside waiting for them, watching the world go by. After about 20 minutes of waiting, feeling more annoyed than bored, I went inside the shop and stood near to Muriel, when suddenly I felt as if a book was reaching out to me. Without even looking at it I went to the counter and paid 25p for it, then I asked, rather irritably, how much longer they were going to be.

We left, enjoyed the rest of our day together, and when we got home I pushed the book into the back of a cupboard.

It was some months later that I unearthed it, and felt the need to go through it. To my amazement there was a picture of an Indian called Red Wing, and believe it or not, he had the nose of a Greek person. Well, I was truly excited — here in this book, which is called Touch the Earth, and which has recently been reprinted, I was looking at the face of a man I had not seen, but yet felt I knew very well indeed.

I was to take a service shortly afterwards, at Fleetwood Church, and so I took the book along with me, hoping the two men who claimed to have seen him would be in the church. When I arrived I found, to my excitement, that they were there, and so I simply asked them to look through the book and tell me if they recognised anyone. I then left, as I did not want to influence them in any way, and when I returned some time later they both pointed to the picture of Red Wing.

What a day that was, what a time to celebrate — I cannot prove to you that Red Wing is the voice I hear, but somehow I feel sure he is. What I do know is that "my voice" always tells the truth, always offers positive advice, never lets me struggle for too long, and always makes me feel safe and secure whenever and wherever I work.

As I travel around I find I form instant friendships with people, and one of these people is a man called Steve, Stevie Baby to his friends. The paths of Steve and I used to cross very often, and still do, but I had been visiting his home town of Blackburn for many years without us being able to sit down together and just chat. Steve invited Ursula and I to dinner on December 29th, 1995, an invitation we were happy to accept. However, when the day came Ursula was not well enough to go, and so Steve and I took the opportunity to get to know each other.

Steve is so easy to be with, he is fun, and cares greatly about people, despite his health having been very poor all his life — Steve is just Steve and everyone loves him.

We set off on our journey to a nearby Chinese Restaurant, and from the minute we met to the time we said our goodbyes some hours later, we never stopped talking. During the course of the conversation I mentioned the story of Red Wing, and Steve became very excited, as he too had been given the name of his guide as Red Wing.

I cannot prove to you that it is the same guide, nor can either of us know it is, but we were rather thrilled to think how often our paths had crossed, how much we felt we had in common, how much understanding of each other we had, and we have wondered many times, could it possibly be because we are of the same soul group (people who have similar tasks in life, similar needs, and similar things to learn) and because of this could we have the same guide — a Spiritual parent to both of us, thereby making us feel a little more that we truly are part of the same Spiritual family?

After all, there must be some reason, surely, why people like you and I meet, and then feel as if we have known each other for all of our lives, feel that we can confide in each other things that we have never spoken of to anyone else.

Maybe the hand that guides could be the voice that guides, not the ultimate power in our lives that we call God, but someone appointed to take care of us, to help us to learn, and to understand the purpose of us being here, through the many experiences we must have. There are so many questions, and each answer provokes more questions — truly an exciting quest.

In the next chapter I will discuss the wider feeling about the personalities that guide us, particularly when we knowingly work with the Spirit world and the workers therein.

MY GUIDE SAYS

This is such an over-used expression, particularly by those people who are keen that others should know that they work for the Spirit world.

Every person on this earth who loves other people and who has compassion and understanding for the needs of others works for Spirit. It is merely that there are those of us who work constantly, and knowingly, proving to people that this is what we are doing. We do so in the name of the truths that the Spirit workers wish to proclaim, mainly that there is no death, and therefore we need to know more about our lives and why certain circumstances affect us individually. We also feel we need to know of the personalities who guide us in order that WE have a reference, so we know that we are communicating correctly.

Guides, helpers, inspirers, higher minds, friends — these are merely some of the names used by mediums, healers etc, to establish for those people listening that they have guidance from the unseen world.

Our helpers do establish themselves with us, individually, in many different ways. For example there are healers who are never aware of the hands that guide them, and who feel no difference at all when giving healing, no transference of thought from the Spirit world, no increase or decrease in heat. They are truly the unsung heroes, because to have blind faith is not always easy.

It is, however, the proof of the pudding as the old expression says, that confirms whether healing is taking place or not, and only the patient can know if they are feeling better. For the healer to be told, later, that the condition of a patient they have treated IS improved shows that there must be Divine guidance, and this is the only encouragement the healer needs to carry on.

In the case of clairvoyants there is the subjective, or objective vision, which can support any information being imparted to a recipient. Sometimes clairvoyants see their own helpers, but many times they do not.

Those people who hear Spirit, clairaudients, may "hear" subjectively the voice, that voice actually being no more than an inner thought, and yet, through the additional benefit of clairsentience they will come to SENSE the personality of the voice that guides.

It is of wonderful support to know who guides us, but not vital to the transferring of information — more actually for the benefit of the medium or healer. What we need constantly is PROOF, PROOF, PROOF, and it is not for the mediums to know what the necessary proof is.

When we accept that as physical human beings we are not the knowledge, not the message, but merely the passive messenger, we will all enjoy our stages of development more, will allow those in the Spirit world who truly guide us to get on with their business, leaving us a little more free of the worry of whether or not the information is correct, rather concentrating on knowing that we are properly prepared to receive and subsequently deliver correct information.

Our guides and helpers will prove themselves in as many ways as necessary to give us greater confidence in us as the transmitters of their knowledge and information, but let us remember that they are never known to say they are greater, better, or of higher knowledge than any other helpers. Sometimes developing mediums, in their enthusiasm, may be known to utter such nonsensical remarks. That is the way of the human mind, not the way of Spirit.

Know yourself, learn to know the personality of the guide who guides you, and having proved to yourself that the guidance is good and knowledgeable, be content to be the instrument, not the conductor of your orchestra of Spiritual understanding, and you will enjoy the experience more.

SEMINARS

THE FAMILY GATHERINGS

It has been a part of my work for Spirit during the past 18 years to bring other mediums together in order that we, collectively, should share our knowledge with those people needing to learn how to understand their own Spiritual gifts.

Having needed answers to my questions, and finding no-one truly willing to share their knowledge, and finding it sometimes a little difficult to afford to go to seminars outside the area, I decided the best way would be for me to organise events, and bring people nearer to my area.

Therefore, I approached a local Spiritualist Church, explained that I wanted to hold a seminar, and asked would they be interested in hosting it. A committee meeting was held, and they thought it would be a good idea. Thankfully, their then President, Anne Lewis, was a very forward looking lady. Without her encouragement I would not be doing the work for Spirit that I am today.

I booked the mediums, arranged a programme, and very quickly people from various parts of the country who knew me and my work planned their journey to the north west coast. We stayed in a local guest house, which we called Fawlty Towers. The food was less than basic, the rooms even worse, and it was freezing cold. When it came time for our baths and showers there was not enough hot water for one bath, let alone enough for all of us.

One of the mediums actually searched the building until he found the central heating controls, where he discovered that everything was on the absolute minimum. He very quickly altered it, and soon we were a little warmer and had hot water.

We had bed, breakfast and dinner there, which meant leaving the guest house to go up the road to the church to take the various classes, do demonstrations etc, and all of this we did quite gladly, as we were so happy to share our knowledge with those attending the seminar. The only thing required of the church committee was that they provide lunch for the mediums, plus morning coffee and afternoon tea for everyone attending. All proceeds from the weekend after expenses were given to the church.

The following year in February 1991 it was again arranged to hold a seminar. The guest house had been booked 12 months previously (thinking maybe it was better to stick with the devil we knew than try somewhere else). However, when I went along to remind the lady of our bookings, I found the place closed down. Apparently she had sold out to someone else, and had not given them any advance bookings.

Panic almost struck but, thankfully, I had enough faith in the world of Spirit to know that if they wanted us to hold this year's seminar, then it would go ahead. I made enquiries in the area, and discovered that a hotel, which was on the promenade, had been newly refurbished, and they had enough rooms for everyone which, of course, I booked immediately, with a sigh of relief.

All could go ahead now, couldn't it?

Wrong again, for I had not counted on it being the middle of winter, and being by the sea I had no concept of the weather in other parts of the country. Luckily, the husband of one of the mediums, who was living in Worcestershire at the time, felt sure that if she didn't set off on the Thursday, in readiness for the Friday start, she would not make the journey. She duly packed, and thankfully arrived late Thursday afternoon — I say thankfully because on the Thursday night there was a heavy snow-fall, which meant most of the roads were blocked. Some people, including a medium, were due to arrive from Leicestershire, and nobody could get in or out of that county.

We woke on Friday morning to discover that other areas were also affected, and in total I "lost" two mediums and nine of the people who had booked in.

Never one to give up I sat quietly and asked my "voice" what should I do, as many people would still be able to come, and I only had one medium plus myself, which was hardly fair to them. I was told to call a local medium, which I did straight away, and as he had no bookings he was able to come. We had an enjoyable weekend, and were simply all very grateful that the weekend could go ahead as planned, with a few minor changes.

I received a letter of thanks from the President of the church, who acknowledged how grateful everyone was to have had the weekend, despite the adverse weather conditions.

I was especially grateful to the mediums during this weekend, because they were so willing to step into the breach. Our bonus was that there, unlike the rest of the country, the sun shone beautifully and we could, after our work, sit in the little hotel and see the sun shining on the sea, almost like a summer's day.

PAST TIMES (REVISITED)

Having so enjoyed organising the weekends, and knowing that the people attending, who travelled from various parts of the country where knowledge was not easily accessible to them, were anxious to repeat the experience, I arranged for another weekend seminar the following year.

This was to be the last one I held at the church as, sadly, the church officials were not pleased about mediums being put up in hotels. I did wonder where they were expected to stay but simply, as usual, handed over the profit from the weekend.

For about 18 months I did not organise any seminars, but little by little, the people who had attended them asked more and more often when was I going to do another one.

One day, Muriel and I went along to St. Annes, and "for old times sake" as we put it, we decided to call at the Lindum Hotel, St. Annes, where we had, in the past, enjoyed some of the seminars organised on a twice-yearly basis. The moment we arrived I was greeted like a long lost friend by the people on reception, who also happened to be the family who owned the hotel. How lovely, we thought, to be back — and then another member of the staff, one of the directors, walked through the lounge and said "How lovely to see you. When are you coming back to us — we have missed you". I turned to Muriel, and said "Do you think this is meant to be, should I make enquiries about holding a seminar here?".

We discussed the matter over lunch, and then I approached the people on reception, and they were absolutely delighted. I said I would hope to have 60 people attending, and they gave me a price, and the rest, as they say, is history.

Of course I immediately contacted the people who had attended the previous seminars, and many of them promptly booked in — and I am happy to say that this event has become the Spiritual event of the year for those attending.

Since organising the first one there is a nucleus of people coming every time, who pass the word to people they meet. I have never formally advertised because I fill the place without advertising, but each year more and more people come, more and more mediums are happy to work with me, and more and more money is being donated to charities each year.

We have, during the time I have organised these seminars, helped the local hospice, Booth Hall Children's Hospital,

Manchester, Children First Charity, Compassionate Friends, plus many Spiritualist churches.

I can honestly say that organising the seminars is the highlight of the year, for the people attending have come to love each other so much, and they always welcome newcomers. We work hard, and we enjoy our play times, during which we hold sing-a-longs, social evenings, and enjoy listening to some of the talent of those who booked to join us — people like Steve, a special friend to all of us who, despite terrible ill-health, sings for us, entertains us, runs discos for us — we couldn't enjoy our times without him.

GRIEF IS PERSONAL

For some unknown reason, many people do not seem to understand that to know of the presence of Spirit means you can also enjoy the normal things of life, such as I have talked of — how sad. We will always miss the presence of our loved ones now in the world of Spirit, but what would be the point of our lives if we never had any fun — surely it is better, in their memory, to show to them that we can cope, can get on with our lives, and by doing so we can encourage all people who come into contact with us to know that, in time, they too will come to terms with the loss of loved ones.

No-one ever "gets over" the loss of a loved one, but we all come to the point of acceptance, and if we can come to terms with that loss and manage, on a day to day basis, to function as normally as possible, we show by example how others may learn to do the same.

I am happy to share with you the story of little Val, a dear friend of mine, who a couple of weeks prior to one of our February seminars lost her beloved husband Richard. She was heart-broken, and yet being Val, was aware that she was responsible for bringing two other people in her car to the seminar, and without her they had no transport.

She telephoned me and we discussed the situation — I felt sure that it would do her good to come along, despite knowing that her husband's funeral was to take place a day or so before the start of the weekend. I re-arranged her bedroom, in order that she could have her own privacy whenever she felt she needed it, and along she came.

I took the liberty of asking two lovely ladies, both of whom are widows, to keep a gentle eye on her, and if she looked as if she needed help, would they please give it. Of course, both agreed, knowing how she must be feeling.

How strange then that throughout the course of the weekend, each time I had five minutes to myself, there was little Val — I got quite used to bumping into her, and each time would give her a little hug. I remember very well the Saturday evening, which was to be a social occasion after the day's work. It was about 9.30pm and I could finally take a little time just to sit and enjoy the company of the participants — wonderful, I thought. Just as I was about to sit down, I saw on little Val's face such a vulnerable look — she was sitting next to a friend of mine. I asked my friend if she would move along a little, sat next to Val, and before I knew what was happening I reached out to her, she fell into my arms, and promptly fell fast asleep (with a little help from two little tots in a glass , I hasten to add!).

One and half hours later my neck and arms were so stiff I could not move, and so very gently friends took her to bed, but not before we had our photo taken, something I treasure to this day.

It was about two years after this that Val was hosting me whilst I was in her local area doing church services, and we talked of how strange I found it that I was the person she wanted cuddles from, not the ladies who had experienced the loss of their husbands. She explained, very gently, that at that time in her life she did not need to hear about other women's loss, or anything they may say about how she would accept, begin to feel better etc, (remember her husband had only had his funeral a couple of days before). She needed, at that precise time, to nurse her own wounds, and to be allowed to grieve. She is a medium herself now, and has had enough proof of the existence of Richard, in the Spirit world, but mediums are human too, and we do miss our loved ones, and so need to grieve in the same way everyone else is does.

What a great privilege she bestowed upon me that weekend, allowing me to be the person she could trust with her emotions, and what a wonderful friendship we have.

She wrote to me, and through her letter asked me to thank all the people at the seminar who had allowed her her own space, and the following year she publicly thanked everyone, saying she could not have got through it all as easily without their support.

What a wonderful testimony to those attending, many of whom come with deep needs of their own, but when in such a happily Spiritual environment they, like we all do, find it easier to cope, to manage and to be strong, no matter what the problem.

UNEXPECTED ENCOURAGEMENT FROM SPIRIT

Having organised many weekends, which were for the general understanding of the various aspects of mediumship, the workings of the Spirit world, and the mechanics of mediumship, I felt it would be rather interesting to organise a special weekend, to concentrate on a particular aspect of the work.

I remembered having met, some ten years previously, a wonderful lady called Ursula Roberts, a trance medium who Muriel and I had met whilst we were attending a seminar at St. Annes.

On this particular occasion Muriel and I were asked to miss a lecture in order to be company for Ursula. Not really wanting to miss the lecture, but not daring to say so, we agreed — and how glad we were we did.

We were, at that time, sitting in circle with three or four others for my development, which was coming along very quickly — what a wonderful group of people they were, all patiently and willingly giving their energy in order to help me to develop my gifts of the Spirit.

During the previous few weeks it had been decided we should sit in the dark, and there should be much singing, and jolly times were to be had. Quite honestly, I do not like to sit in the pitch black, because I have sometimes wondered if true phenomena is always taking place, and on two occasions I found that the people purporting to produce phenomena were actually faking it. Therefore I became more and more uncomfortable.

Muriel, that evening, did something so unusual I could not believe it. We had often discussed the need for mediums, when not working, to be allowed their rest periods, and yet here was Muriel pumping Ursula Roberts for information regarding our circle. Ursula listened patiently for some time, then turned to me and said very quietly "My dear, I take it you are the medium of this circle?". I admitted I was. "Well", she said, "I can tell you that only if you, the medium, are happy with all that is taking place , will the Spirit people be able to work as they wish to".

(We went back to our circle the following week, and I said I was not happy sitting in the dark, nor with the singing, and we changed things and our group work for Spirit became much stronger).

Before the weekend ended Ursula Roberts did a demonstration of her trance mediumship, and I can honestly say if I never again saw anyone do such a demonstration it would not matter, for the things I saw with her that evening were so wonderful I still feel emotional when I think about it, all these years later.

I sat at the very back of the room during this demonstration, and was overwhelmed when I was allowed to witness the full processes of the entrancement — her guide Ramadan drawing very close to her, and then speaking to us and then asking if we had seen anything. He felt this would help the understanding of his medium to know how much those attending had witnessed. I vowed to myself that I would keep quiet as I did not want to appear to be a "clever clogs" but eventually, having listened to the things other people said, when Ramadan asked again if anyone had seen anything I stood up, and immediately I began to speak I felt the tears roll down my cheeks. I had seen things that evening I had never seen before, but which to this day have remained as a memory of the true trance state — and during his reply to me Ramadan encouraged me to believe in the current stages of my own development. Muriel and I discussed the evening well into the night, and could not wait to get to our circle the following Thursday.

And so here I was, some years later, thinking about holding a seminar which would have greater interest for those attending, particularly those wishing to understand trance mediumship. I sent out a thought to Spirit, and hoped that Ursula Roberts would be willing to come along.

A short time later I was working in London, where on two occasions during a four day period I bumped into Ursula Roberts, and the following week she happened to be at Portsmouth, which I was visiting a little earlier than I needed to in order to spend time with Lotte and Ernie, friends you will hear more of later.

By the third meeting I "got the message" and so I asked Ursula if she would be willing to come to St. Annes. She agreed, but not in the winter months as she still drove her car, despite her great age.

I arranged to do a seminar the following August, told people what the subject would be and it is one of my greatest sadnesses not to have not been able to fulfil my hopes for that weekend, as sadly Ursula passed to Spirit before the set date.

We did, however, go ahead, kept thoughts of Ursula and her wonderful way of working in our thoughts, remembered her personal approach to discipline, and enjoyed a wonderful few days together.

Sometimes it is difficult to accept that the plans we make don't turn out exactly as we want them to. We need to learn to be very flexible — to accept we do not know ALL things, no matter how psychic or mediumistic we are. To be rigid does not allow us to accept the natural flow of psychic and Spiritual energy, of which we are all a part.

It is also important for us to accept that no-one is indispensable — there is always someone else to fill our shoes, take our place, take other people's knowledge forward. As I say so many times — we are not the message, merely the messenger, and if we remember this we will enjoy what we are intended to do, and accept that which we won't do with grace, instead of condemnation of others.

MOVING HOME

I WILL SURVIVE!

Do you ever wonder why you have met some of the people who are in your life? Has it ever been proven to you WHY some of the events which have taken place in your life happened?

I have had so many instances that I worry about boring people, because every day, it seems, there is another situation to report, but one of the latest ones is something I have found so amazing I will tell you about it.

The story itself concerns my move back to my home county of Lancashire. After the break up of my marriage, and having spent two years living at my mother's with my mum and step-father, I realised it was not fair to continue to stay with them, and so, once again, thoughts went out for somewhere of my own to live. An opportunity presented itself which enabled me to move to South Yorkshire, where I was able to rent a newly built Housing Association flat.

It was a wonderful way to prove to myself that I could survive, because I knew no-one in the area at that time, but sadly I did not enjoy actually living there, never feeling it was my home.

After seven years or so I had definitely had enough, especially as I found that, whenever possible, I was staying with Ursula, and enjoying the company of my friends in Blackburn. All my social times were spent with them, we celebrated joint events together, and of course, Christmas was not Christmas if it was not spent in Blackburn.

I applied to the Housing Association for a transfer, applied to the Council, tried as many ways as possible of getting a transfer. In the midst of all this I was being told, in various parts of the country, that a medium from Lancashire was busying himself about my business, and that in fact he was telling all and sundry that I wished to move back to Lancashire for a variety of reasons, none of which were true. The most ludicrous and untrue part of this was that I had bought a house in Blackburn — how I wish I could, I thought!

I became so upset about his foolish remarks, and his interference in my business, that I phoned him and told him I wanted to hear no more of it.

I continued my search for alternative accommodation, spending less and less time at my flat.

A MOVING STORY

One day in January 1998, a friend phoned me and said he knew someone who was going to sell a house, and that he thought it would sell for a very fair price. I went along to the bank immediately, knowing that I would not be able to have more than a tiny mortgage, and having no means of finding a deposit, and got the information I needed.

To please my friend I arranged to visit the house as soon as possible and, having seen it, was told the selling price. It was far beyond my reach, I knew, and so I told the vendor that I was sorry to have wasted his time.

During the next few weeks so many strange things happened — Blackburn Council wrote and asked if I was interested in renting a two bedroomed house, despite my having been told there was no way they could offer me anything as I had no "points" (I know nothing of their points system). Strangely, the houses they were talking about were all a few minutes from the house that I had viewed. Everything seemed to be pointing me in the same direction.

Through a strange set of circumstances I was encouraged to seek the help of a mortgage broker who, even though I didn't qualify said I could have a mortgage. Another friend then swung into action, on my behalf, and I began to see a real pattern of help unfolding. What struck me as very strange was how everything I did all pointed me to the same place, in the Blackburn area. Other mediums began to give me messages saying I would be moving very soon and so, although nothing seemed to be moving very quickly I felt sure that, behind the scenes, a lot was happening.

I further realised that all the people who were giving me so much help and guidance were all people I had only met during the previous two or three years, except for Steve who started the ball rolling by phoning me in the first place.

In May of 1998, not knowing when I would be moving, yet feeling sure I would, by Christmas, have my own place in Blackburn, I began to move my belongings to Lancashire, a car load at a time, and another friend, who has a storage warehouse, offered to store everything until I moved.

So much of a positive nature was happening that I had to believe that I was being helped, over and over again, and on September 5th 1998 I moved back to Lancashire, to the house I had first looked at in January 1998. Amazing? Yes it is! True? Yes it is!

I wonder to whom do I owe my thanks? There are so many people I could not begin to thank each one, because I am sure I would miss somebody out — I only know that I was obviously meant to have this house. It is my home and everybody who comes to visit says the same thing — how cosy it is and what a lovely atmosphere it has.

Jean, the previous owner, was in a home for the elderly, whilst her beloved home was being sold to pay the state for taking care of her. She passed to the Spirit world just a few weeks before I actually moved in, and each time I change something, to suit my own needs, I feel obliged to tell her that I am not changing it to upset her, just because I want to make it my own.

Imagine my joy when, a week after moving in, and having decorated the living room pale green, I was given a message by a medium at a demonstration from Jean to say how much she enjoyed and loved green. I also began to wonder, at that time, what she actually looked like, because from first having moved in I had been aware of a small red-headed lady, but then my own mother was just 5' tall and a red-head. However, I knew it was not her, and so I asked a neighbour, and her cousin who had sold me the house, what she looked like, and I'm happy to say I now have some photos of her. This little red-haired lady with whom I share my home!

We should remember, always, that nothing is real, or not as real as we make it seem. After all, Jean loved her home, but when she passed to Spirit she left it behind. Now I live there but one day I shall also pass to Spirit, and I can only hope that the next people to live in my home will feel the love and joy I feel each time I go through the door.

My eternal thanks to the chain of people, seen and unseen, for bringing me home!

SPIRIT CALLING

A STORY TO MAKE YOU THINK

Some of the private sittings I have had have truly been remarkable, and one in particular really stands out.

In 1984 I booked a sitting, for his March visit, with Nelson Ross, a wonderful auragraph artist who had been trained by Harold Sharp. Although I had never seen Harold Sharp I had seen his beautiful drawings, and I had seen a demonstration by Nelson Ross.

In 1984 I had been sitting in private circle and was receiving much information from Spirit which I was able to pass on to people, and was actually taking church services. However, I had very little confidence in my own abilities, and although I KNEW that what I was receiving was correct, I found myself having many sittings, each time hoping for further encouragement from the higher minds in the world of Spirit.

I was very excited as I was going to St. Anne's, where Nelson Ross was doing the auragraphs. He was at the home of Dorothy Rogerson who was, at that time, on the committee of St. Annes Spiritualist Church.

As I walked into the room Nelson looked up, then turned away and took a piece of paper from a selection which was at the back of the room. I now know that he had a few standard designs, which he coloured in according to the information and directions coming from his Spirit advisors.

The sitting began in the normal way, with Nelson drawing, explaining what the colours and symbols meant, and family and friends from Spirit popping in, also. During the course of the sitting he mentioned trance work, something I knew nothing about at that stage, and yet he insisted that I was a trance medium. After denying this a couple of times, he further explained something which WAS happening during my development, and gave me advice about it, saying that it was always best to test the information, and giving me some pointers as to how to go about this.

I duly left Dorothy's home, and immediately I got home I put the tape in the machine, as I had found that I remembered very little afterwards, and yet when I heard the tapes again I remembered everything.

To my disappointment, there was absolutely nothing on the tape. I telephoned Dorothy to enquire whether anyone else had had a problem with their tapes, to which she replied that no-one else had reported a problem, and then she suggested that I merely kept the tape, because she had discovered that this sometimes happened, and yet the information was forthcoming at a later date.

I put the picture away, and put the tape with the others I had kept and forgot all about it, until the July of that year when, through a very strange set of circumstances, I found I was able to go to Stansted Hall for a week's seminar.

At this particular time in my life, as I have previously mentioned, I was unhappily married to a man who constantly felt threatened by anything and everyone I spoke to. Consequently, the only place I was "allowed" to go was to my circle, at Margaret Thorpe's in Blackpool, once a week, and to the church. During June of 1984 Margaret told me that there was a vacancy on the Blackpool week at Stansted, a very popular week organised by Betty Wakeling, who also organised a bus to take people down to Essex. Of course, I told Margaret there was no possible way my husband would allow me to go, but she said I should ask him. His only response, on this occasion, was to say that we had no money for me to go. With all the confidence in the world, and knowing there was a bare fortnight before the week, I said "Spirit will provide the money". I had not the knowledge or understanding of the workings of Spirit at this stage, so had simply said what I felt to be true, and true to my prediction all was well. The phone never seemed to stop ringing, with people requesting sittings, and by the end of the two weeks there was exactly the right amount of money — £89 for the course, plus the bus money. This was probably the first time I really felt able to acknowledge the incredible workings of Spirit, despite having had many such incidents happen, most of which I had simply taken for granted in the past.

I began packing in readiness for the trip, when my "voice" told me to find Nelson Ross's tape. Of course, I thought, I would need old tapes to tape over, as I wanted to record as many lectures as possible, and that particular tape was useless, wasn't it? However, my voice further instructed me to listen to the tape, which I did (I never refuse to listen to this particular voice — his is the voice of my soul, I believe, and has my interests truly at heart). Imagine my absolute amazement when I heard the voice of Nelson Ross as clearly as he had spoken on the day of my sitting almost four months previously!

I listened very intently and realised that some of the aspects of my development, particularly the "trance" he referred to, had not started taking place in March, but by the time I heard the tape in July they had begun. Amazing? Incredible? Only when you have never experienced such happenings. Quite honestly, the more you involve yourself with trying to understand the workings of the Spirit world, the more such events prove themselves to you as quite natural and normal.

CONTACT RE-ESTABLISHED

During the next couple of years I tried to have a further sitting with Nelson Ross, but on each occasion he was ill, and I was very sad to hear, during a visit to Don Galloway's week at Stansted in the autumn of 1986, that Nelson Ross was ill, trying to support his elderly mother, and was having some financial difficulties. Immediately on returning home I telephoned Dorothy Rogerson and asked if a demonstration could be held at St. Anne's Society meeting place, and if all the proceeds could be sent to Nelson Ross. Dorothy agreed on condition that I was the medium. I replied there was no point asking me as I was a local medium, not very well known at that stage, and so I felt people would not pay to come. However, she insisted (and no-one argued with Dorothy), the evening went ahead, the hall was full, and a donation of £100 was sent to Nelson Ross — not such a great amount today, but adequate in 1986, and every penny was donated with love. I took no fee, of course, and the friend who drove me to the church took no travel expenses. It seemed little enough to do for a man who loved his work for Spirit, and who had given so very much to so many people.

A follow up to this story may interest you. A couple of years later, I was working for Don on a Lynwood Fellowship week, and a young Dutch woman I had previously met, but did not know very well, booked a sitting with me. During the course of this Nelson Ross made his presence known to me, and asked me to tell her that he was sorry she would not be able to receive her usual auragraph. She confirmed that she knew what he was talking about. He further gave me reason to believe that he knew her personally, not just as a medium to a sitter, and she told me that Nelson's brother lived in Holland, and that whenever Nelson visited her brother, she and her family met up with him. Nelson then showed me a beautiful picture, and I told her that if I had crayons and paper, under his direction I would be able to do her an auragraph.

Since that time Nelson Ross has periodically made his presence known, and has confirmed through other mediums that he is willing to help me to do auragraphs. Sadly the pictures I do are not artistically very good — something I discussed with a lady who hosted me when I was visiting Otley Church — "Oh", said she, "Do you want to see some of Nelson's early auragraphs?". She duly produced some pictures, which absolutely amazed me, for they were as basic as the ones I was doing. She then told me that Harold Sharp had trained him, and I thought how very fortunate he was.

I am occasionally aware of the presence of Nelson Ross, and ever grateful for it, as I know other people who have benefited from his help and guidance since he passed to Spirit. How wonderful to know that our special gifts do not die with our physical bodies. Nelson left a great legacy, for he had been ill for so many years, and yet he always showed how much he enjoyed his work, something we should always remember to do, for the work we do with and for other people is such a joy, such a challenge, and such a privilege.

IS THERE ANYBODY THERE?

There have been numerous occasions when I have been contacted, spontaneously, by someone in the Spirit world, and I would like to share some of those times with you. I realise it may be a little difficult for you to understand how this happens, and I do not have all the answers, but these things DO happen, and on each occasion someone else has been there to witness the events, almost as if the Spirit communicators want more people to acknowledge the truths of life after death.

Anyway, one such occasion was during a visit to Baton Rouge, Louisiana, a place I came to have a great fondness for, due to my having made such good friends there, during the past seven years.

I was staying at the home of a lady called Susan, and one morning was having an in-depth discussion with a friend, a young lady from the locality who is a massage therapist. Suddenly the door bell began to ring persistently — I knew nobody could be ringing the bell because we were sitting directly in front of a large picture window, and nobody had approached the house. However, as the ringing did not stop, I mentally asked what was going on, and immediately I heard my mother's voice saying "Phone England" over and over again. I relayed this to my friend, and together we went to the front door to check what had happened. The door bell was pushed right in, and so we pulled it out and, of course, the ringing stopped. No sooner had we sat down and resumed our conversation before the persistently ringing began again.

This time I was very angry and said to my mother, who of course was talking to me from Spirit, that as soon as we had finished our discussion I would ring England — and I can tell you I was not very gracious about it. The ringing stopped straight away.

Having concluded our time together I telephoned my sister, as I could think of no other person who my mother would want me to telephone in England, and as soon as we spoke my sister, who was quite distraught at the time, said that she had been asked to collect her young teenage daughter from school, because she had been drinking whisky and was very drunk.

Of course I told my friend about this, and we analysed the reasons for my mother asking me to make the telephone call.

Firstly, when she was still alive she always worried about my sister, and this particular grand-daughter.

Secondly, my mother thought that alcohol was something evil, and so on two counts she was given cause for concern.

I further concluded that I, being so receptive to the voices from Spirit, was the only person who could have listened and then carried out her wishes. Furthermore it was of great help to my sister to know that whilst she was so worried, mum was still watching over her and caring about her troubles.

So often we find that people, having passed to the Spirit world, continue to react as if they were still here. My mother always referred to my sister as "poor Shirley", believing that she couldn't cope (as so many parents do), and therefore constantly worrying about her, and it would seem that she is merely doing exactly the same now in the Spirit world.

THE DETERMINED SPIRIT

At this point I think it may be of interest to those of you who wish to analyse some of the stories I am relating, to know of the events of my mother's death some seven years ago.

Three weeks before she died I was in the United States with Linda, my good friend, and we were visiting Boston, she for work, and me simply accompanying her and enjoying the sights of Boston whilst she worked.

During our time together I became increasingly worried about my mother, so Linda insisted I telephone home to speak to her, which I did. She was very breathless, and complained of the heat, something she did not normally do. However, during that summer there were some heat waves, and she assumed it was just that.

A couple of days later I telephoned again, and she seemed worse, her breathing being very difficult, but this time she said that she had put pesticide on all the plants in her large bedroom, which she used as a greenhouse (she had about 350 small potted plants), and that she had then closed herself in for a couple of hours, and so she just assumed that she was having some allergic reaction.

The third time I phoned I was very worried, but she would not go to the doctor, she said, because if she did she knew he would tell her she must stop smoking, and whilst she had cut down considerably, she could not envisage life without her cigarettes. However as the heat was also still bothering her very much I insisted that her husband go the next day and buy her an electric fan.

I was due to leave the United States a week or so after this, and just a day or so before I left a most peculiar letter arrived from my mother. She summarised her whole life, quite bitterly insisting that no-one had cared about her, that everyone had always wanted to take everything away from her, etc. I was horrified, mainly because none of it was true, just imagined by her negative state of mind, something that had dogged her whole life.

I read it to Linda and then said I would not reply but I would go to visit her when I got home. Thankfully mum had ended the letter by apologising for "off-loading" onto me, saying she simply felt better for having got it all out of her system — she had just needed someone to know how she felt.

Having decided to do nothing about it at that time, I was just putting it away somewhere safe when my "voice" said I was to sit down, immediately, and reply to the letter, and that he would help me to find the right words.

Of course I did as I was told, and I will always be grateful to my inspirer for his insistence that I reply, because I never saw my mum again.

As I was writing to her I realised that I was not writing as a daughter to mother, but as a medium to a client, something I found easier to do. My mother and I had had a difficult relationship, for reasons I choose not to go into, but during the last couple of years of her life we had become closer, and I know that my letter will have helped her.

A few days later I left America, arrived home, and as I was unpacking I put to one side all the things I had bought for mum. Amongst them was a jazz tape from New Orleans, and Linda had given me an Elvis Presley tape for her (my mother adored Elvis, and would sing his songs every day).

MUM'S FUNERAL

After being at home a couple of days I prepared to go, as a guest, to Don's Lynwood Fellowship seminar at Castleton in Derbyshire, and I spoke to mum on the phone before I left. We had a somewhat strange conversation, because she told me she knew what music she wanted to have played at her funeral — it was a New Orleans Jazz piece, something that was always played when the black people of New Orleans led the funeral procession through the streets. She opened her mouth to sing the particular piece of music and simply said, with horror, that she had no breath to sing. My immediate reaction was sadness because every day of her life my mother sang, to lift her spirits I expect, and now she was telling me she couldn't sing! We concluded the call with me saying I would call to see her in a week's time, I would bring the jazz tape, and she could tell me which piece she wanted. After all, she was only 62 and so there was plenty of time to plan her funeral, wasn't there?

How wrong I was!

You know, sometimes the most mediumistic of us do not know what is going to happen, particularly in our own lives, and especially when our emotions are involved.

I enjoyed a wonderful few days with Don and the Lynwood family, so many people who had become part of my extended family — Gee, Reta, Toni, and so many more, many of whom are now in the Spirit world.

On the morning of the 24th July, at 5.40am at Losehill Hall where the seminar was taking place, I suddenly woke up to hear fire alarms going off, and so immediately dashed out of bed, down the stairs, to find everybody else doing exactly the same. After a short time no fire was discovered so we re-entered the building and went back to bed.

Please note the time — it is truly relevant!

The day proceeded as normal, with lectures, classes etc, but I was quite restless, and so I went into the village, and enjoyed time just being with my friends. In the evening I played scrabble for a little while, and then decided to go to bed early, something which was quite unusual, but I thought I was still suffering from jet lag.

I had only just undressed, and was about to go to bed when there was a knock at the door and a young man who worked at Losehill Hall was standing there. "Val, there are two people from the police wanting to talk to you", he said, and for some ridiculous reason I thought someone was playing some sort of joke. He assured me there really were two police officers downstairs, and so I quickly went down to see them.

Their words will remain with me for ever — "Someone in your family has died, and your parents are too upset to talk about it. You must phone Linda Weidner in Pennsylvania and she will tell you what has happened". My only thought was that something must have happened to my son, if my "parents" were too upset to talk about it, especially as my parents were divorced, and both re-married.

I went straight to the public call box, and thank goodness a friend came with me.

Linda answered the phone straight away and said she couldn't quite find the right words. Feeling quite ill I said "Just say it", and she said "Your mum died this morning".

I heard a scream but did not realise it had come from me. From that time all is a little blurred but I remember people taking hold of my hand, of my friend finishing the call, and of being given some medication by Paul, a herbalist, and shortly afterwards I went to bed, and actually slept very well.

The next morning I telephoned my sister, and she told me that mum had passed in her sleep, with no signs of stress, and that the time had been gauged at around 5.40 am — THE EXACT TIME THE FIRE ALARM WENT OFF!

Mum had always had very strong psychic energy, but I think that sometimes it frightened her. I remember some of the times when she was in her shop and things would suddenly literally fly across the room — thankfully things such as wool and cotton wool packets!

I have absolutely no doubt in my own mind that my mother, at the precise moment of her death, was reaching out to me, to let me know she would be all right. A very unhappy woman in life, I know she looked forward to the next life with relish. I, of course, will always regret not having seen her for the last time, but I must accept that was the way it was meant to be.

How I have laughed, so often, thinking of my mother needing to let me know she was about to make the most important journey of her life. Knowing that I sleep very deeply she had to find some very dramatic way of waking me up. Nothing was found to be wrong with the fire alarm system, and as a follow-up to this there were many incidents at my sister's house during the next few days of electrical interference, something she has attributed to my mum and her particular brand of psychic energy.

One of the last instances of mum making her presence known was when I took her sister to visit my father and his wife (my parents had a very bitter marital break-up, and never healed the rift with each other). We stayed a little while, reminiscing about old times, and as we were leaving having a final chat on the door step, when suddenly a car on the roadside starting flashing its lights and making a dreadful noise. Yes, of course, the alarm was going off, but no-one was nearby at all. It belonged to someone who was staying with my father, and he began looking for his car keys, when just as suddenly the noise stopped and the lights went out again.

My father's comment was that mum was probably very annoyed that I had taken my Aunt Valerie for a visit — strange comment from a man who claimed not to believe in such matters, but I feel sure he was quite right.

ARE YOU LISTENING?

One other such incident occurred on 23rd December, 1997. As usual, as I was then still living in Rotherham, I was spending Christmas with Ursula in Blackburn.

Ursula's family have become like my own family, and we were very much looking forward to Christmas. On the evening of the 23rd Ursula was to prepare food for a family Christmas Eve party, and I had to prepare a programme for a funeral I was to take on Christmas Eve for the mother of another friend.

We had dinner together at about 6 o'clock, during which someone from Spirit made their presence known but, knowing I had such a heavy evening ahead of me, I said it was not the right time and would they please go away. Ursula has reminded me of this occasionally since then, because it was rather an unusual thing to happen spontaneously. I am very disciplined about my work, and the Spirit people respect this.

However, this was just one such event on that particular evening. Almost immediately afterwards a loud noise came from the hallway. Of course we investigated, to find that a carrier containing Christmas presents had toppled over. However, this could not account for the noise as the contents were soft and very lightweight — another puzzle.

After dinner I left Ursula in the living room, and proceeded to do the programme for the funeral service for the following day. After typing for about an hour I went to ask Ursula if she would listen to what I had written and tell me if she thought it would be suitable. As I came out of the bedroom, where I had been typing, I saw the bathroom door open but no one was there, as Ursula was in the living room. There was no draught, and even if it had been a windy night, there was no through air which could have caused this to happen. When you open her bathroom door it does not move freely, because the floor is carpeted.

Something is happening, somewhere, I said, but I don't know where!!

Having discussed the funeral service I went back into the bedroom, finished it, then put my things away, thinking that we had become so very serious we needed a light-hearted moment or two. In the corner of the bedroom I saw a hat I had bought when I was in Canada with Lotte (she had bought some of them for her grandchildren, also). It was made from a red fleecy material, with two ears and the face of a cat on it. I put it on, and what a peculiar sight I looked. White night-shirt, black tights and a red hat with face and ears, and I made a grand entrance into Ursula's living-room — she nearly fell off the settee she laughed so hard!

"That's it", she said, "I must get a photo of this" — to which I replied "Well, if you are taking a photo you must do it properly as Lotte did when I stayed with her". She found me a shawl — (this was a particular joke between Lotte, Ernie and I). For some reason I always felt the cold when at Lotte's and so one day, to shut me up, she had given me an old grey shawl and woolly hat, then taken a photo.

As Ursula took the photograph there was an almighty crash from inside a narrow cupboard in her living room. I can assure you that no-one had been in that cupboard all evening. Only the toys she kept for her grandchildren visits were in there.

"That's it", I said, "Something has happened and I need to know what it is". Now, friends know that if they are worried, or really in trouble, I may pick up on the situation but I do not always know who the thoughts are coming from, and so they know they must telephone my home and leave a message on my answer phone, and when I am concerned enough I will phone home, no matter where I am in the world, and retrieve my messages.

I dialled the code and listened to the messages, nine of which were just the usual type, wishing me Happy Christmas, however the tenth was from Ernie, and I am sure I will remember his words to my dying day. He said "Oh, hello Val, this is Ernie. I just thought you should know, Lotte was not feeling very well, the doctor has been and they have taken her away in an ambulance". My heart felt as if it had leapt into my throat, I yelled out, and poor Ursula wondered what on earth was happening. Immediately, I telephoned Ernie and asked him to repeat what he had said in the message. It still did not sink in, and so I said "Are you telling me Lotte has passed to Spirit?" and of course, the answer was "Yes". I burst into tears, Ursula took the phone, Ernie cried, and so the call ended.

On reflection I feel there is so much to be learnt from all the events of that particular evening. You need to know that Lotte and I had only returned from a visit to Vancouver, Canada, at the beginning of December, that I had then spent a week with her and Ernie prior to going back up north, that we had many plans made for the following year, so very much to look forward to.

Many people thought we were sisters, both being plump, middle aged, fair haired people, and we used to joke that we were, but our joke was that she talked strangely (she was Danish). The bond between us was incredibly strong, and I loved her as dearly as one would love a sister.

We had discussed the workings of the communicators from Spirit in great depth, and Lotte was more concerned with the mechanics of mediumship, the work behind the scenes, than she was with individual messages. Spirit need more people like her — people who will ask questions and test and test again.

WHEN SOULS ARE BONDED

Because of the close bond between us, she would want to let me know what was happening, for she cared about her family more than anything else, and I know that even as she was journeying on her thoughts would be for those she would be leaving behind.

I have to ask myself, and so should you, why was there such a lot of activity that evening, activity that could not simply be ignored? Why would Ernie telephone me so soon after Lotte passed? I phoned home exactly half an hour after she died, and the precise moment of her passing was when I was talking about her, having the photo taken which so reminds me of her, and that was followed by the crash in the cupboard.

Some things, in my opinion, cannot just be ignored — if there is a real living intelligence behind such situations don't we owe it to them to investigate as much as possible? Some people would find a means, I am sure, of trying to convince me and people who have experienced similar events that we should dismiss such happenings as coincidence, but are they coincidental? You must judge for yourself, but I ask you not to just ignore such a catalogue of events if they should happen to you, BUT, at the same time, do not attribute each and every seemingly strange action to those in the Spirit world.

We need balance in everything and we need proof, for we are trying to establish a dossier of truth — to what purpose you may ask?

It has been my privilege to ask questions of Spirit communicators on many occasions, and to be part of many reunions between Spirit people and their loved ones still on earth, and each and every contact proves to me that there is genuine purpose behind all communications.

I have spoken to many intellectuals on the subject, many of whom have taken the time and trouble to analyse situations which are sometimes dismissed by those who are afraid to investigate further. The general consensus of opinion is that there is an intelligence behind such communications, their purpose being to establish life after death, which in turn gives purpose to the lives of those left behind, for they know they must journey on eternally, and therefore the life on earth is merely a place to grow, to evolve, in the best way possible.

If we are to believe that the good that we do is noted, by some higher force, we must also accept that any negative actions or thoughts are also noted, and for so many, KNOWING that they are watched over and guided by loved ones, now in Spirit, encourages a better way of life.

After all, using a personal example, I loved Lotte on earth and wanted her to think well of me, and so that continues, for I try to order my thoughts and actions in such a way that she, and others who care about me, will not be disappointed in me.

Think about it, and make up your own mind!!!!

SPIRIT PEOPLE CHOOSE THE 'RIGHT' MEDIUM

Before I close this particular chapter, I realise that some of you may wonder why you have not had the evidence you have wanted, sought and waited for, and so I relate to you a quite astounding incident.

Some 12 years ago I was taking the Sunday afternoon service at Hyde Spiritualist Church, and during the course of the afternoon the doors were flung open, and a young man and young woman entered the church.

I do not take kindly to people disrupting services which are already in the stage of clairvoyance as this one was — I was actually in the midst of giving someone a message whilst this was taking place.

However, I made no comment and simply carried on giving the message, when suddenly I was aware of a man from Spirit pulling me away and insisting that I give a message to the young lady newly arrived in the church. Without even giving me time to argue with him, (our communicators, remember, really are living personalities) he gave me a lot of evidence to offer to his daughter, with reminders of memories, birth dates, proof about his passing, in fact all the usual type of evidence.

It was only after the service that I realised the full implications of his message, for his daughter came to me and thanked me for the message from her dad. She further told me that she didn't understand why he had chosen that particular time and day to come to her as, during the previous 12 months, she said she had spent £2,000 visiting mediums and having private sittings, none of which had established communication from her beloved dad. I heard myself explaining that we cannot, no matter how much we spend, buy time with our loved ones, that they actually choose the time, the place, and the medium. Stranger still, she had no plans to be in the area that particular afternoon. She lived some distance away, but her boyfriend was attending a singing competition in the town that evening, and he remembered having previously visited the church, so thought she might like to attend a service there.

We ended our chat by concluding that her father HAD obviously chosen this particular situation to prove a point, to which she added "And today is his birthday!".

I cannot fully express on paper the excitement I felt at this stage, or the privilege I felt at being chosen, by her dad, to be the medium who would give her his messages of love. The whole situation only proved to me once again that if we offer ourselves in service to those loved ones in the Spirit world, they will find the right place, right situation, and right people to promote their truths. Simple isn't it?

I can only hope that those of you who are still seeking, and still needing to establish real contact with YOUR loved ones will eventually do so, in the most simple, yet astounding way possible, but in a way that brings peace to your heart and to your mind.

BE CAREFUL WHAT YOU ASK FOR

GETTING EXACTLY WHAT YOU ASK FOR

Have you ever wished or prayed for something, and been surprised when you have received exactly what you asked for? Sometimes we need to be careful, for we may get exactly what we want, but do we want it when we get it?

I have found that, especially during difficult times, I ask God for help, and more I and more I am realising that what I receive is EXACTLY what I have asked for, but not necessarily what I intended it to be.

One such instance is quite funny, the other quite incredible I think, but I leave you to make up your own mind.

About six years ago I was working for the Lynwood Fellowship with Paul a herbalist who was very kind to me, and who tried to help me regarding some health problems which I had had for some time. Don suggested that I should spend time at Pauls clinic which he ran with his wife, and that I would receive exactly the help I needed in the right environment.

As part of the treatment I was given home-made fruit juice, which as well as being good for me was absolutely delicious, particularly apple and celery. How I would love to have a juice extractor, I thought, but at the time there was no possible way I could afford one.

During my visit mutual friends came to stay, and it was decided that we would all go to a car boot sale nearby. "That is where I will find myself a juice extractor" I said. I say things like this all the time, sometimes not knowing why I say them, but it is usually right, without any conscious thought behind the expression of the words.

A group of us duly arrived at the car boot sale, which was set up in the local marketplace. Looking on every stall I was very disappointed not to find a juice extractor, when suddenly one of our group shrieked "Here it is — the juice extractor!". When we saw what she was holding up it was not, as I had expected, a rather grand and modern version of an electric juice extractor. Oh no, it was a tiny thing in a 3" x 1" box, probably from about 1950. On the front it says "Juistractor" with instructions on how to extract the juice from the fruit. I just had to buy it and have, on occasion, taken it along to lectures to use as an example of how, when asking for something, we really need to be quite specific.

GOD THE PROVIDER

With this thought in mind, at the end of 1998 I was unable to work, due to health problems. Having been lent money to see me through the first month, the second month's bills were piling up.

Just before Christmas I was invited to lunch by some wonderful friends at St. Annes. They actually live almost opposite the Premium Bond building . As I was passing I expressed a thought or wish as follows, "Please God, do you think that Ernie could give me some money, even if it is only £500". (You probably know that the nickname for the Premium Bonds computer is "Ernie").

Immediately on arriving at the home of my friends, I told them of my conversation with "God", and having done so promptly forgot about it UNTIL...

At the beginning of January I received quite a lot of mail, and in one of the envelopes was — yes, you've guessed it — a cheque for £500 from Ernie. However, this was NOT Ernie from the Premium bonds, but Ernie, Lotte's husband. The accompanying letter made me cry, because he said he realised that I must be worried about money as I was unable to work, and had only started paying a mortgage three months earlier, and he knew me well enough to know that I could not stand being in debt, and that therefore I would probably start to work before I was fit enough.

(Two days earlier I had woken up, and thought that was exactly what I must do, because bills have to be paid, don't they? I had been selling personal things to pay some bills, but that could not go on forever, and so something would have to be done).

What an amazing way for a prayer to be heard and answered. Ernie and I laughed when I phoned to thank him, because I told him how he had been used by the Spirit world, in order to help me. I could almost hear Lotte saying "go on Ernie, you must do this, because Val really needs it".

REAPING WHAT YOU SOW

REAPING WHAT YOU SOW

Do you, I wonder, believe that everything you give away is returned to you when you need it the most.

I could actually write a whole book on how events have proven this to me during the course of the last 18 years, since I stopped taking things for granted, and began investigating the workings behind the scenes.

During one of my regular visits to Lotte and Ernie a couple of years before she passed to Spirit, we were discussing one of their grandchildren, a beautiful, articulate little girl, who had just been categorised "unteachable" by the education system. Lotte was absolutely horrified, having had similar problems when she was a child in Denmark (and I can assure you Lotte the woman was an incredibly intelligent person!).

Her concern for the child moved me very much. Some time later I heard that the little girl had been taken to a school where she was assessed, and the people there were sure they could help her to speak properly. However, this was a private facility, and would cost £1,100 per term, and she would need to go for two terms.

Lotte wanted to help, and I realised there must be some way I could help too. I had no money to give but I do have gifts, which I use in my work, and sometimes it is wonderful to be able to help people by using these particular gifts.

I therefore approached various church individuals to ask if raffles could be held, the money to go to the fund to help a little girl be "normal", and I arranged to do public demonstrations, all the money going to the fund. Friends helped, taking part in demonstrations with me, and during a period of about ten months we raised £2,222, enough money for two terms.

I well remember Lotte saying that Ernie couldn't believe that I was willing to do so much to help a child I did not even know, but to me, it seemed little enough to do for people who had opened their hearts and their home to me.

And now here was Ernie, helping me in a way that was so wonderful it gave me peace of mind.

Money should be seen simply as an energy, which can flow freely for ever, helping where it is needed, and always flowing in the right direction. Nothing can be gained by storing it up and never letting it see the light of day.

I can only speak for myself when I say how overjoyed were the parents of one little girl, by the help they received for her, and the support they felt at a difficult time, and how grateful I will be, forever, to Ernie, for returning the favour when it was needed the most. The amounts of money are totally irrelevant — what is relevant is that prayers were heard and answered!!

DECEMBER 1981 – INSPIRED PHILOSOPHY FROM 'MY VOICE'

I wish to tell to you a philosophical tale. There were three men of equal intelligence who all became very rich at the same time. The first man surrounded himself with possessions and adornments. The second man became a recluse, spending neither on luxuries or necessities, but spending a great deal of time counting his fortune. The third man supplied his family with their needs, and on rare occasions gave them a special treat, whilst a great deal of his time and money was spent on the underprivileged, the orphans and those in mental institutions.

Now which of these three men would you say was the most fulfilled?

Number one simply gave himself all the trappings of the rich to show to others that he WAS rich.

Number two lived a peculiarly unreal life, always fearing his fortune may be wrested from his grasp.

Number three, on the other hand, realised he had more than he required and was willing to share his good fortune with others, thus creating new relationships and friendships.

How truly rich was this man in all aspects of his life — his family were happy, his new-found friends were happy. So my friends, I say unto you, keep enough for your needs, allow yourself a little luxury, but be assured of a different type of wealth when you are able to give happiness to others.

It is not always necessary to give of your material belongings, a word to the lonely, an ear to the distressed, a prayer for the desperate, is all it takes to bring a greater understanding.

IS THERE ANYBODY THERE?

COMMUNICATION — WHEN THE RECIPIENT ISN'T PRESENT

One of the most remarkable aspects of my work is when loved ones in the Spirit world manipulate and manoeuvre those of us on earth to ensure we are in the right place, at the right time, to receive their communications.

There is a mistaken belief that those who communicate from the Spirit world can only do so when their own loved ones are able to receive the messages they offer.

In fact, they very often choose to give messages of proof of survival of death to friends of their loved ones, for therein can lie greater proof, and the prompting of many questions, don't you think?

One such incident, among many others, proved to me how, given the right circumstances, the right medium and the right recipient, a message of absolute proof of life after death may be produced — even though when the message was being given the recipient was actually many miles away.

I was taking a Sunday morning church service at Portsmouth Temple, a lovely church, and on this occasion the service was downstairs, something that is a tradition once a month, allowing those who have walking difficulties an opportunity to enjoy a service. (Most of their services are in the beautiful church upstairs).

During this seemingly unremarkable service, a lady from the Spirit world communicated to me that she wanted to speak to Margaret. Of course, I asked if there was someone in the church called Margaret. No response, a medium's nightmare! However, having double-checked with my communicator I asked again for the name of Margaret, this time giving more information.

This time a lady sitting at the side of the church put her hand up, and said she knew Margaret and felt sure she knew the identity of the lady communicating. From this point very personal proof was given which established beyond doubt that this was indeed the mother of Margaret, a friend of the recipient. Before moving on I simply asked if the message could be conveyed to Margaret as soon as possible.

The proof of the truth of this particular communication was, unusually, received later that very day — I arrived at the church for the evening service and was introduced to Margaret, by a lady who has, since then, become a very close friend, a friendship based on mutual love and respect. Anne, the lady in question, had telephoned Margaret as soon as she got home after the morning service, and relayed the message I had given. Margaret was amazed for, having recently lost her beloved mother and feeling particularly depressed, she had gone to visit the cemetery, and was praying very hard for help, at the very time her mother was communicating with me. Margaret in London, and the communication being received in Portsmouth. Amazing? Incredible? Somehow I don't think so — I rather think that there is something so normal about this, but that we don't understand exactly what is happening or why.

Maybe if we investigated a little more thoroughly we would understand more and more. The Spirit world offer us many challenges, sometimes in the form of communications, but do we, perhaps, just take this a little for granted — do the messages have to be so obviously unusual for us to sit up and take notice? I hope not, for each message is a message of hope, and of truth — if you have not been able to prove this for yourself yet, I hope you will investigate, and establish your own particular knowledge, and having gained that knowledge I hope you will share your stories with other people, who may be trying to find their own belief system.

For mediums such as myself who work continuously for the Spirit world, travelling from church to church, town to town, and sometimes country to country, it is sometimes difficult to evaluate our own work, for we do not often receive feed-back and yet, like any other job of work, we need to know if our standards are as good as they need to be.

I am, therefore, always very grateful to those people who do take the time to let me know when a contact has been particularly evidential, and one of those people was Anne, who I have just mentioned.

I had done a private sitting for Anne, and on 21st August 1995, Anne felt the need to write to me, to give me confirmation of some of the evidence contained within that sitting. What a kind gesture — I offer to you her exact words:

"You referred to Renee — Renee was a lovely lady, a lifelong friend of my mother's. She became my friend on my mother's passing. She and Dick (Anne's husband in the Spirit world, who had already furnished her with proof through my mediumship) liked one another a lot. The last time Dick was fit to go out was spent in Renee's garden. She was devastated when he passed. 18 months later she was in a similar condition to Dick, and through his suffering I was able to talk to her about death, and I think I may have helped her to die peacefully. So for me to know they are together and jointly looking after me gives me great comfort."

Apparently, during the same sitting, I gave Anne proof of the presence of her mother, and said that she was very sad about young people going to war. Anne further enlightened me as to the proof of this when she told me that her mother was widowed when Anne was two, in 1942, and yes, she said, he was in the RAF.

The proof of a communication is for the recipient to determine, and people like Anne are not gullible, as many sceptics would suggest. They actually are very intelligent people who knew their loved ones well, and would not, for one minute, accept proof purporting to come from those loved ones if it was incorrect.

She is one of many people who, during the past 18 years of my working with the Spirit communicators, have helped me to understand my Spiritual gifts better, because the communications do raise many questions. Why don't those who communicate simply say for example "My name is Joe Bloggs, and I was 72 when I died, and I passed in a hospital in Newcastle, having lived at 10 Broad Street"? I wish I knew all the answers, but I do not — I can only surmise that by giving us a small portion of the whole the rest is up to us — just a case of meeting them half-way. By doing so we open many memories to the past, some of which are happy and pleasant, and some not so pleasant, but which have left behind emotional problems which we may need to deal with.

THE TAPESTRY

Thinking of Portsmouth reminds me that Lotte was absolutely wonderful at anything to do with sewing, knitting and especially cross stitch. I actually have a little tray cloth that she originally bought from a car boot sale; a lovely embroidery she was finishing that somebody else had obviously started. Suddenly she gave me one of her crafty sidelong looks and said "If you were to have such a cloth as this, what colour thread do you think you would like to join it all together?" I mentioned that I would like to have the green of the leaves as that would pull it together nicely. When my Christmas present arrived that year the minute I picked it up I knew what it was. I phoned her straight away and said "When I open this I know exactly what it is". Lotte was like that.

Whenever she gave a present she would spend a long time making it and want to make sure that the person really wanted it. She felt there was no point in giving something that they didn't want.

I had bought for her, at her request, the chart that was the head of an Indian chief in cross stitch which she was going to do for a friend of ours, Don Galloway. One day when I arrived to see her it was about half done and she held it up and said "Guess who this is for?" and I said "It's for me". I never assumed anybody would do something like that for me. She just grinned and said "Yes that's right, I will do Don another one when I have finished yours". It's magnificent. I have it now and it is so beautifully done that you can see the texture of the feathers through this cross stitch. I put it in a lovely blue frame and will always treasure it. Lotte could just look at a chart and know exactly where the stitches had to be. She could adapt and adopt anything.

I saw a fabulous chart one day which could take two or three years to complete. It had three dream catchers and feathers and in the bottom right there was a beautiful Native American saying. I said to Lotte "I would love to have that!" and she said she would do it for me. She bought it, took it home and put it in a chest of drawers which was full of these types of things that 'one day' she was going to do. She passed last year and none of them had been done.

However, last January (1998), shortly after Lotte's passing, I went to Castleford Church for an Assessment associated with one of my Spiritualist National Union certificates, part of which was a regular service. When I came to the place in the service to give a message I gave the surname Fletcher and asked did anyone know this name. The other communications had gone very smoothly and I was very relaxed, but this one was sticking. When it sticks the energy doesn't flow, I know it's not correct and it's not the right person. That is very difficult, but suddenly I heard "Dyecast

Engineering" and knew I didn't know what that was. I further said somebody in the room knows the surname Fletcher associated with this engineering company. A young woman said "I know about that" — I gave the message, some situations and a link was established with her mother in Spirit who had loved her children very much. At the end of this particular message session the people who had received the messages were questioned by the assessors regarding the relevance of the information.

A young medium I had previously met called Marie had been sitting with the young lady and during the time the young woman was being interviewed by the Assessors Marie came to me and said she had to give me a business card. The card was in the name of Fletcher at Dyecast Engineering! The message from her mother was for the young woman and her brother who was the Fletcher who owned the Dyecast Engineering company. Marie then said when the woman returned from the Assessors she would talk to her about me mentioning that she liked sewing, which she had denied during the communication. The girl came back, at which point Marie said "You told Val that you don't do sewing but you are forever doing tapestry and cross stitch!", which prompted me then to tell the tale of Lotte buying the diagram of the three dream catchers and the Native American saying. She went as white as a sheet and said "Three years ago I bought that exact tapestry and I have never known why and never knew who it was for and now I know it's for you. I will do it for you one day. It will take four or five years but I will do it for you".

Since then Marie has written to me letting me know that Carol is doing it and when it is complete she would like to frame it. Also over the last year Marie has received brief communications from Lotte. She always passes them on — the last one being quite remarkable in its evidence and personal nature. How wonderful that I was talking about Lotte in a service, linking with the young woman and her abilities and the beautiful tapestry. Some people may dismiss this as pure coincidence but why? It is important that we don't take everything for granted. Often Spirit will give us messages and it is important that we recognise the synchronicity of it, and the way it all comes together. It is so beautiful sometimes.

Postscript — On the 3rd March, 1999, I was in Copenhagen, Denmark, doing a demonstration of mediumship. After the demonstration I was very pleased to see two nieces of Lotte, and behind them was Lotte's sister, who I had not seen since the funeral.

I returned to England a couple of weeks later, to find a message from Marie saying the cross stitch was finished and we should get together. We finally did meet in Skipton on the 16th April, and it was then that Carol told me that she knew she had to hurry up and finish the work by the 3rd March. What she didn't know (having worked very hard on it for 14 months) was that I would be in Lotte's beloved Denmark on that day, that I would be meeting her sister that very evening, nor did she know that, on the following day, the 4th March, it was my birthday. What a fabulous birthday gift — it is so beautiful, and so much love has been put into it, that I could cry each time I see it. BUT the greater joy is knowing the hand that Lotte played in making sure I got it at exactly the right time.

1997/98 – A TIME OF LEARNING HOW TO LET GO!

CANADA — 1997

In November I went to Canada, where I was to work for the International Spiritualist Alliance for the whole month, serving various churches, and doing private sittings. Joyce Tarvin, the president of the association, hosted me, together with her husband John, both English born people who emigrated to Canada in the 1950s, and everything was beautifully organised. I worked at some of the spiritualist churches around Vancouver, and also on Vancouver Island, and during that time my lovely friend Lotte came to visit her long-lost school friend.

Quite amazingly, when Lotte had first tried to find her friend, after many long years of not knowing where she was, she placed an advertisement in a newspaper in her native Denmark, but didn't hear anything. Some 18 months later she received a communication from someone who, having been ill, had been reading some old newspapers, and he contacted Lotte with the news that her friend was actually living in Canada. Meanwhile my friend Jill, having moved to Vancouver, had contacted Joyce Tarvin, mentioned me and so the process to book me was started. The strangest thing of all was to know that Lotte's friend and my friend actually lived a couple of blocks away from each other in a suburb of Vancouver.

I thoroughly enjoyed my work, meeting new friends and discovering the joys of working with people a different culture, who nevertheless, having come from England, had taken British mediumship to Canada, and promoted it beautifully, retaining all the good old standards. The challenge of a new environment was fantastic, and on Vancouver Island I did a demonstration at a Cowichan Indian Village, in the Long House, which was hired by the Duncan Spiritualist Group, led by Minister Pat Gunn.

The evening was incredibly well attended, having been efficiently advertised by the church, and was followed by my taking the church service the following morning. I was amazed to note how many people from the demonstration had said they would attend the church the following day, as I did not know the size of the church, or how many people it held. What actually happened was absolutely incredible, because when Pat and I arrived, about 20 minutes before the start of the service, the church was already full, and people were beginning to form a queue outside in the rain. I was taken upstairs to spend a little quiet time before the service, when someone came in and asked Pat what they should do, as so many people were wanting to come in and the place was full. As we were in an upstairs room of what is actually a local community centre I suggested that they ask everyone to bring up their own chair and we would take the service upstairs. Each person carried their own chair up — one lady had to be brought up in her wheelchair, the organ was carried up, and in five to ten minutes we had recreated the church and the service went ahead — a most enjoyable experience, and proving, once again, that the place is irrelevant, for the people are the church!!!

TYING UP LOOSE ENDS

Lotte and I had very little contact during the month I was working, but flew home together, talking incessantly about our different experiences and when we got back to England her son Christopher met us with her car. My memory of the journey from the airport to her home in Hampshire is of sleeping, but for one minute opening my eyes to see heavy snow and registering the scene as a winter wonderland.

We arrived at her home, where her husband Ernie had lit candles, Danish style, which provided a beautifully comforting atmosphere for us to walk into, and the house was filled with flowers.

We had about six days together before I drove back up north, and that was the last time I saw Lotte alive. On December 23rd, having spent the day preparing food for what was to be the Danish Family Christmas, on Christmas Eve, and then having watched a TV programme she had been looking forward to, Lotte passed quietly and peacefully, in her own home, exactly as she had said she would like to. The shock of her death is something I don't think I will ever come to terms with, and whilst the evening's events leading to her death are quite phenomenal from a psychical research point of view, from a personal and emotional point of view I feel sure that the stress contributed greatly to my serious health problems, seemingly triggered by a fall which happened in May 1997.

A MEDIUM IS ALLOWED TO GRIEVE

In total this year I have lost four friends, and it has made me wonder if perhaps, as mediums, because we are expected to always understand death and why it occurs, we ourselves forget to deal with the normal emotions that affect us all. I can speak for myself when I say that Lotte's passing, more than any other in the past 18 years since I first started understanding my mediumship, has taught me that we need to give time to our own grieving process, and that no matter how much we understand that our loved ones are now suffering no more and are surely enjoying their new stage of progression, as human beings we are left with a loneliness and an emptiness that needs to be dealt with properly. No matter if that means shedding tears, screaming and shouting, asking questions of our Spirit friends we need to NOT put our grief to one side. It we do we are simply suppressing it and at some future date other situations can occur which simply add more stress to a possibly already stressful situation.

After Lotte's death I cried every day for a month, and only after I had taken a memorial service for her at Portsmouth Temple did I begin to feel a little better. The service was not about death, but about the life of a lady who was special to many people, and the President and committee of the church very kindly allowed their lovely church to be used, and even provided a beautiful tea for all those attending.

LOTTE'S OBITUARY

Lise Lotte Henriksen James nee Mogensen — 17th July 1941 — 23rd December 1997.

Lotte James was a remarkable lady, often to be seen during Lynwood weeks, sitting quietly in the background somewhere, seemingly caught in her own thoughts, actually missing nothing but enjoying everything.

Her first Lynwood week in Essex was a turning point in her life, for she had experienced much phenomena, and fearing for her sanity, was inspired to go to Clacton, not knowing what to expect.

Meeting Don, Reta and many of the Lynwood family, and being welcomed, helped her to understand herself, her Spirit contacts, and made her feel truly at home with herself. She always said "I am not a spiritualist – I am a Lynwoodian".

Lotte and I shared many private conversations, and during those, Lynwood was always mentioned. One of my last memories of her, upon our return from Canada, is of us listening to a tape she had made of a Lynwood concert which she would listen to frequently, and we could be heard, by her husband Ernie, singing "Let there be peace on earth" which she had first heard during a seminar.

Lotte passed, very suddenly, blissfully knowing nothing and now knows the reality of the spirit world, something she investigated in every way possible. Never content to be TOLD anything she listened, dissected, and then drew her own conclusions. Lotte was very much her own person, intelligent, articulate, and truly non-judgemental — an example to us.

Since her death, many people have expressed their sadness, for she will be missed — her simplicity, her strength, but above all the true joy she transmitted whenever 'Lynwood' was mentioned.

We practised together the song 'I have a dream' which speaks of Angels, and believing in seeing good in everything we see — that for me, epitomises the Lotte I knew — she came, she gave and she loved, unconditionally. In her memory, may we try to do the same.

FRIENDS IN SPIRIT

In early 1998 I received a phone call from someone from the Fleetwood Sea Cadets asking if I would be willing to do a fund raising Evening of Clairvoyance at the base for them. Due to past connections I said yes and Muriel agreed to chair the meeting. Amongst those attending were the Atkin sisters and their mum Edith, a lovely lady who I had originally met around 1984, and whose home I had visited several times.

Edith was a sick lady for most of the time I knew her, and eventually it was established that she had Parkinson's disease amongst other health problems. How sad, for she and her John used to love to travel — they had a wonderful family life, all their children loving and respecting them, and I used to love my visits to do private sittings for them. After each visit Edith used to do me a tea cup reading, which was always accurate — in fact she was the first person, ever, to tell me I would visit the USA, EVEN pinpointing which area.

Anyway, back to the story, Edith had apparently been housebound for 12 months, prior to coming to the Sea Cadet base, but when she knew I was back, visiting the area, she insisted that her girls get her in the car and bring her to the demonstration. Little did I know this would be the last time I would see Edith. She received a communication towards the end of the demonstration, and of course I took a little time to have a chat with her, and a hug.

The following week I wrote to her, saying how glad I had been to see her, and her daughter Susan telephoned to thank me, but also to tell me that her mum was in hospital, so they had taken the letter there, and had put it on the wall for her. At this stage she was very ill, so Susan took my mobile telephone number to keep me in touch with what was happening to Edith. I was actually in a Chinese restaurant, in China Town, Birmingham, when I received the news that Edith was very poorly indeed, and shortly afterwards she passed to Spirit. Our only comfort is to know that all her restrictions are gone, and strangely, her illness and subsequent passing have brought her daughters and I back into close contact again, something we had lost when I moved from Lancashire to Yorkshire. I will never forget Edith, a loving mother with a wicked, but wonderful, sense of humour.

DORIS

Another person I had more and more contact with during 1998 was Doris, a lady I first met at Stansted in 1984 — she remembered me as a young woman (I was 36) and apparently acknowledged to herself then that I would "do well" as she called it. Periodically we would have contact, and then about three years ago she wrote to me, and that was the start of a regular correspondence. I still have some of Doris's letters, and many were very funny — her observations of life were very satirical and incredibly descriptive.

About three years ago she wrote and said that her John was quite ill, and needed many tests, for arthritis and other associated problems. This started a terrible time for them both, with Doris spending most of her time worrying about John and his health. Sometimes he received treatment at the local hospitals, and other times he was hospitalised, as a means of giving her respite. All of those who knew them, for they had attended my seminars, sent absent healing, in the hope that it would help, and wonder of wonders, one day I received a letter saying the doctors were absolutely amazed, as he was so well, and could they attend the February 1996 seminar. Could they? — I was thrilled, and so were all the others I told. Consequently Doris and John received lots of extra attention, healing, love and hugs during that seminar.

Sadly, shortly after they returned home his health deteriorated again, but morale had been boosted, so they coped. In the middle of 1997 Doris's letters changed, becoming more sad as she tried to cope with John's illnesses and the thought of losing him, and when, finally, he passed to Spirit in January 1998 she was sad, but at the same time relieved for him. Having lost her beloved son many years ago, and having researched this business of life after death, she realised that at least he was no longer suffering, and so she made herself busy, thinking of the many things she would do just to keep her mind occupied. HOWEVER, just two weeks later, she was told she had breast cancer and would need to have the breast removed immediately.

I feel sure that this was the beginning of the end of quality of life, as Doris had known it, for her letters changed again, and whilst sometimes she tried to be cheerful, actually the real humour had gone out of them, and therefore from her. She questioned many things, especially about why she felt she was not coping as well as she wanted to, and actually put a lot of pressure on herself.

One day in July, whilst thinking of final arrangements for the August seminar at St. Annes, I received news that someone who had been given a free place on the seminar was unable to come, and my "voice" said "Phone Doris". When my voice speaks I do not hesitate, and so immediately I DID TELEPHONE HER. She was desperately sad that day and was, even as I was thinking of telephoning, walking around her little garden, sadly wondering about why she was still alive when she was so very sad, and when she only wanted to join her John and her son. I suggested that she may like to come for two days, free of charge, to the seminar but she was so surprised she couldn't take it in. I said I could give her a little time to think about it, but I needed to know as soon as humanly possible. A very short time later she telephoned, said she was still amazed, but that she would like to come. I then found one of the speakers to bring her, because she could not afford the cost of a taxi.

The time duly arrived, and on Saturday morning, Bank Holiday weekend, Doris arrived, very tired, but quietly excited, and after just two hours she looked totally different — happier, healthier and more relaxed, which made her talk, and talk, as only Doris could, reminiscing at double-quick speed, pleasing everyone who witnessed it. She went to bed that Saturday night, tired but very happy, and Sunday morning said she couldn't understand why everyone was so kind to her and so nice. She never seemed to realise that she gave even more than she received, and that she taught us so much about truly coping with sadness, and distress.

On the Sunday evening we had a demonstration of mediumship, and unfortunately the room became very warm indeed and Doris experienced some difficulty with her breathing. As she was to leave immediately the demonstration finished, I announced that she needed a little rest, and that I hoped we could find a nice taxi driver who would take her home, to make sure the house was alright before he left her. John Bescoby, one of my regulars, very kindly offered to drive Doris home, and little Val, another regular, who is used to caring for the elderly, said she would go along and make sure Doris was properly settled in before they left.

A few days later I received a wonderful letter from Doris to say how very grateful she was for everything she had received during the weekend, including the private sitting which Muriel had treated her to. All in all, through Doris attending our seminar, we were all given an opportunity to witness, at first hand, how we may be able to cope if sadness and pain seem to be crippling our lives, and to give her a little something. I was due to go to America on 20th September, and Doris wrote and told me it was her birthday on the Friday of that week. Although I was in the middle of unpacking boxes, and trying to get my house in some semblance of order, having moved on 5th September, I felt it important that I stop what I was doing and go to Doris's, taking her to a local restaurant for her birthday. However, on the day itself she was too ill to go out, so I took cream cakes, went along with a friend, and we had an enjoyable couple of hours together, leaving a very content lady behind.

I went to America and, upon my return found a letter waiting for me, written in stages, in which Doris categorically stated that she was ready to go to Spirit and be reunited with her John. She also enclosed a copy of a poem she had written in 1985, which I thought you may find interesting, for when I heard just a couple of weeks later that she had passed to Spirit, I realised that her last letter had been exactly that, and that it was her goodbye to me.

I will miss Doris, but if she left me with one lasting thought it is that, if in your darkest hour you feel sad, if you try very hard to you can still find something funny to think about.

Doris was typical of so many, one of the world's triers, who felt it was better NOT to let people know how you feel, except those you can trust absolutely not to say anything about how they knew you were playing the game.

Finally, for 1998, there was Mary, a friend I met at Stansted, again, in 1987, just two months before I ended my marriage, after a miserable 19 years. Mary realised how sad I was and when I got home she sent me a photograph of her beautiful garden, saying that if I needed to feel peace I should imagine I was there, and if I could actually go I would be very welcome.

Some months after I left my husband I took her up on her offer and in October 1988 I made my first visit, which was the start of a very close association. I would simply telephone from wherever I was, and Mary would say to her daughter "Penny, empty the washing, she is on her way!".

Mary was truly unique, in every way, stubborn and knowing but very much her own person, her love for jazz surpassed only by her love of the Spirit world and the communicators and communications she had come to know and love over a period of many years.

When I met her she was searching for Spiritual truths more than at any other time, grieving as she was the loss of her husband.

Her daughter, Penny, had been through a difficult time emotionally, so in October 1987 Mary brought Penny to Stansted, which is where we first met, little realising at that time that it was to be a friendship that would last until Mary passed to Spirit.

Mary was a lady of generous Spirit. During the early days of trying to survive on my own it was the kindness of people like Mary that kept me going — her letters were like little booklets of helpful advice, and loving encouragement, always. She would sit in her kitchen at the large picture window, watching the little birds at play, receiving some beautiful inspiration every day, some of it finding its way to my door.

Whenever we were together Mary, Penny and I gelled together very well and Mary and I spent many happy hours together between my work times, putting the world to rights as women do.

For over five years I was a very regular visitor to Patio Place (the name of her home) and then, as life dictates, things change. I stopped smoking, having been a very heavy smoker, and it became increasing difficult to stay with Mary, who was a smoker until the day she died in 1998. We stayed in contact by letter and occasionally saw each other, as our lives changed somewhat.

Mary began to run more groups and circles in her own home, helping people to reach their true Spiritual potential. She was a strict task master, but fair — she had had many years' experience of seeing mediums, listening to them and analysing them, and her words after one visit to a seminar always remained with me: "Well, I've learned how NOT to do it, now I will try to learn how to do it properly".

Arrogant, do you think? Maybe it was, but knowing that something is not quite right makes us want to do a little better, doesn't it? We will none of us ever reach our true potential if we are content simply to be what other people are — we must constantly strive to better ourselves as individuals, and as instruments of the Spirit world, and for the work they want us to achieve with their loving guidance.

What I do know is that Mary helped many people to find their own level, quietly and in the background, wanting and needing no fuss to be made, and like a good mother whenever any of her "children" achieved something and were able to work publicly for and with Spirit, she would sit there very proudly, never claiming credit but knowing perfectly well that they couldn't have done it without her.

Whilst that was not her function for me, she was my listening ear and so many times advised me to "keep out of things" and get on with the work I was supposed to be doing.

Sadly for so many people, during the last couple of conversations we had she remarked how very tired she was feeling, and how she hoped she would not have to sell her house and move. She did not want to have her bed brought downstairs either — it was, therefore, the greatest kindness offered to her, by God, when in July 1998 she passed peacefully in her own home.

Whilst this was a terrible shock, it was good to note that she never had to lose that independence which meant everything to her.

It was with a great deal of sadness, but with a feeling of that I accepted the responsibility of taking her funeral service, at the Solihull Crematorium on July 24th — the anniversary of my mother's passing!

I think it was probably, as befitted a unique lady, quite a unique service — the room was absolutely full, standing room only, and a double slot had been booked for the service (meaning double the time usually allowed).

The first half hour was the usual form of service, with hymns, remembrances by friends, tears as well as laughter, but then after the committal we held a memorial service for Mary, with lots of personal memories, the joyful knowledge that she would now be with her husband Jim in the Spirit world, and we all left there knowing that Mary would be happier now than she had been for some time — and as we emerged into the open air a jazz band was playing one of her favourite songs. We then went along to a local hotel for lunch, where her favourite local Jazz band played throughout the meal — a fitting memorial for a lady who had made her mark in this world, and in the hearts of the many people who knew her.

RED WING
(see page 33)

(BELOW)
VICTOR AND STEVE
(See page 33)

(see page 39)

VAL AND TEDDY
(see page 43)

RETA AND GEE
My two "mums"
(see page 61)

URSULA (see page 65)

PRESENTATION OF TAPESTRY (see page 81)

MY DANISH 'SISTER' LOTTÉ (see page 88)

MARY WILLITTS (see page 93)

(see page 119)

BJARNE VAI AND WENCHÉ, 'DENMARK' (see page 167)

HEALING

During April 1990 I visited, for the first time, the healing group in Harrisburg, Pennsylvania, to which Vonnie Steckel belonged. (I first met Vonnie at Castleton in Derbyshire, England, on a Lynwood seminar. Vonnie had been brought by Linda, which fulfilled a dream for her). This was, I feel, one of the most remarkable groups I have ever been privileged to visit. The people here did not have a set of hard and fast rules, but they allowed total flexibility, and had done for some 20-odd years, never knowing who was going to turn up, but always prepared to keep the door open, and a place for anyone who could visit.

I was collected by Jane, a fabulous lady in her late 60s with such energy that I could never compete, and she explained briefly what would happen — so by the time we arrived I already felt I knew the ladies. I think what impressed me the most about them was their obvious love for each other, a lovely, gentle, caring quality not always found even in the most "spiritual" of groups.

I was accepted immediately, and just as quickly felt at home, although I did wonder what would happen, and would I continue to feel comfortable. Claire, in whose lovely home we were meeting, began by taking us through a meditation, accompanied by music, and then began the process of absent healing, which I have used in workshops many times since that day. We were asked to simply speak the names of the people we knew who were ill, or sad, and who needed help in any way, and as each person spoke, I could feel the energy in the room becoming stronger and stronger, until it felt so tangible it could be felt by just reaching out. We were then asked to think about the countries in the world where there were difficult conditions, and to extend our thinking to incorporate the whole Universe, something I had not tried to do before, but accepting we are all part of the one whole, it made sense.

97

Immediately the circle ended the ladies quickly decided which restaurant they would go to for lunch, and I remember thinking how remarkable that, for so many years, they had met and done such good work, quietly and with no fuss, and they so obviously enjoyed their time together that those who could would always lunch together as well. I looked forward to those events so very much, and through this little group I met such wonderful people.

It was further explained to me that when people were unable to attend the group, prayers were said for them as well no matter how long it had been since they were able to attend.

Looking back to that time now, in 1999, I am reminded by a card they sent to me, on my return to England, of their hospitality, and genuine kindness to me during that first visit. Claire, whose home we visited, has recently passed to Spirit. Also Helen Lee, a lovely feisty lady, passed to Spirit a couple of years ago after a terrible battle with cancer, now joined in love with her daughter who had passed. Never a day went by when Helen did not feel the sadness of losing her daughter, and so I now rejoice for her, whilst still missing her. Noreen has been involved with healing for an incredible number of years, and no doubt continues to link her thoughts to the healers in the Spirit world, and the wonderful Jane never ceases to amaze me. I visited her home last year, and despite her own pain, she gave me the most wonderful massage — she always reminds me that she is quite elderly, but I just wish that I had the enthusiasm for life that Jane does, and the generosity of Spirit that she has. She has truly been one of the people who has taught me the most.

You know healing is not something you need to learn — you simply need to feel it, and it is not always about healing wounds. One day I was with Jane, and we were at an outdoor car boot sale, on a blistering hot day. A little girl was screaming the place down, and we discovered that she had been at the sale with her mother the whole day, and she was obviously tired, hot, and very weary. Jane simply looked at the little girl, with her dirt blackened, contorted face, and said "What a beautiful little girl you are" and immediately her little face lifted into a smile, and her eyes were for Jane, and Jane only — that is what I call the magic of love — for Jane recognised the little girl's needs and responded to them in the most Spiritual way possible.

I shall love her always, for she lives as she speaks, and always feels that she has more to learn, something we all know but don't always truly believe.

FATHER VAL

I came to realise, a long time ago, that having said to Spirit that I wanted to serve I had to leave myself entirely to those workers in the Spirit world, and try not to interfere.

On occasion I have wondered why on earth I didn't try to make more of a bargain, but since I did not, I have come to know that the Spirit workers will always point people in my direction when there is need, knowing that I will not refuse to help.

Such an occasion occurred when I was working at Rugby Church in the West Midlands, a church I have worked at happily for many years now, and where I feel very much at home.

A letter was handed to me, which rather surprised me, as nobody knew I was actually there, and the mystery continued when I saw the address on the envelope "Father Val Williams" — the letter read as follows:

"Dear Father. Could you please help me. I am desperate and have tried everything. I do not know what it is singing horrible. It does not come on in the day at night, some tune Daisy Daisy, & God our help, and also Onwards Christian Soldier, this is what was sung at husband funeral he died Christmas Day there is only one

person who I told was her next door so how does anyone know the tune sometime Father it goes on at 4 in the morning I had the doctor last week and he said to me if anyone is playing these tunes. Sometimes it is louder and then it goes on quiet I have tried to say it is in my mind I have done everything prayed morning and night 6 weeks it has been going on I am on tablets a day but I told the doctor they don't seem to work He told me to keep on with them I am not mad father but now there is only one hope and that is healing which I do believe in I have a bad heart condition and believe me Father I am trying very hard to get well this has only happened since he died last six weeks I keep saying what is it I written to the Doctor on ITV but he never answered my letter I am sure if I have healing it will help me.please help me Father I have worked all my life and I was in RAF this war never had anything like this before. I have never been to Rugby I have only lived here 5 years to my sorrow, please forgive me writing to you but the church is my last hope. Thank you Father and God Bless you. I live in old age pensioner bungalow and I am 72 years old . My phone number is.........."

Luckily she had put her full name, address and telephone number on the letter, and so I asked the people at the church if they would contact her.

This was not, unfortunately, as easy as we would have hoped, because shortly after this the lady had her telephone number changed. However, now on the track of needing to help an obviously distressed soul, one of the healers from the church went to the address on the letter and there found the lady in question. They, at the request of the church President, Jose, explained that I was merely a visiting medium to the church, explained who and what they were, and were able during a period of a few weeks, to give her healing, and helped to stabilise her emotions. The last I heard she was feeling much better, was not worrying about the music any more, and felt more acceptance of the fact that her husband was in Spirit.

Thank God for Healers. They are simply ordinary people, who come from many different walks of life, who happen to have the necessary love and compassion for their fellow man, together with a need to know how to further their own Spiritual development.

HEALING NEEDS NO WORDS

I have been visiting Denmark since August 1989, and on one of my annual visits, it was suggested that my hostess would take me to Jutland, a beautiful island some distance from Copenhagen where I was staying.

From the moment of my arrival we were both incredibly aware of the presence of Spirit, and particularly of a little boy in the Spirit world who would sometimes give me information and guidance for people. I have known his mother for many years and he and I established good contact with each other some time ago.

It was very helpful being aware of his presence throughout the days prior to the journey, for on the day we were to travel we packed the car, went to the garage and filled up with petrol and began our journey to the ferry. Which was a long distance away. However, we had not even left Copenhagen when the car broke down. The weather was incredibly hot, somewhere in the 90s F, and I was left guarding the car and our belongings whilst my hostess walked to the nearest garage to seek help.

She returned after quite a wait, did what she felt would be the right thing, which had worked many times before, and tried to start the engine again — nothing — absolutely dead, so the only alternative was to telephone the automobile association to which she belonged. During my wait I had become aware, again, of the little boy in the Spirit world, and although he was not communicating any information I knew he must have some purpose for making himself known at that particular time.

The man from the automobile club arrived, could not start the car and so towed us to the nearest garage, where the car was examined and declared to be unfit for the road. The manager of the garage further said that "someone" must have been watching over us because, in that terrible heat, had we driven far with the car in the state it was, there could have been a nasty explosion.

With great relief, although sadness that we could not continue our journey, we ordered a taxi, and went back to her home. I went straight to bed for a rest, but about an hour later she woke me and said she had booked a train, and we were to prepare for the journey straight away.

While I was preparing for what I knew would be quite a journey, I reflected on the happenings of the days since I had arrived — the fact that I knew my friend's son was around so many times, the fact that the journey was being made almost impossible, and quite honestly I doubted the sanity of the woman with whom I was staying, but had not the courage to say I did not want to make a long train journey. Had Spirit told me not to go I would have said something, but nothing was forthcoming from them and so I gave in, not very graciously, and managed to pack just in time before the taxi arrived.

There began a very long journey on the train, the train going on the ferry, a lovely ferry journey and then finally we arrived at our destination. To my horror I discovered that my host and hostess spoke no English, and I spoke no Danish. However, the lady who had taken me would interpret so it would be no problem.

During the visit the son of the house was in need of some healing for pains in his head, so of course I was asked and I gave some to him willingly.

The following day the father of the house asked my friend if I would give him some healing, and so of course again we fixed a time, and I said he should meet me in the dining room at the appointed time.

What happened next was quite remarkable. When I arrived for the appointment it was to find that the man, who knew nothing about healing, had had a shower, and changed from his working clothes into a clean vest and trousers. He was in a mood of excited anticipation, which I could feel, and so I simply asked my friend to tell him to relax as much as possible, and he would probably feel heat from my hands, with the possibility of some vibration. Immediately I laid my hands on him he seemed to zonk out, becoming very deeply relaxed, and the healing proceeded. Everything was reasonably normal until I touched one of his knees and the top part of his leg, whereupon the hand vibrated quite violently (this always happens where the pain is the greatest).

Knowing nothing about his physical pains, and yet trusting Spirit implicitly, I worked on him for some time, and then when the healing was over I was impressed to say that he may feel some discomfort the following day, but that the day after he should feel fine.

The following day I saw nothing of him, but the day after that his daughter came looking for me and asked what I had done to her father. Feeling a little worried I said nothing, just given him some healing. She said the day after his "healing" he felt worse than he had ever felt, but today all the pain had gone from his leg — she then told me he had suffered constant pain in his leg for over 20 years, and in fact his leg always dragged along with pain — but now all pain had gone.

Of course, I was thrilled. I simply asked her to tell her father that we may never meet again, but that should he ever need healing in the future he should sit in the chair, imagine that I was standing behind him again, and ask the Spirit healers to help him.

Some time later I received a report from his wife, through an interpreter, to say that every night he goes to bed, lies down, thinks of me and smiles a very broad smile, and to my knowledge he has no pains since. It was at this point that I reflected on all that had happened since I had arrived in Denmark for what had turned out to be an amazing trip, with so much happening — knowing that my friend's son was so close to us right up to the time of the car being condemned, and thinking about how the manager of the garage had said "someone" was watching over us. I telephoned the child's mother back in England and told her. She was expecting to hear from someone, she said, because she had been told that her son was helping someone in quite a dramatic way.

When this happens it is wonderful to know that we are guided and protected, sometimes from our own foolishness. Imagine what would have happened if we had restarted the car, continued the journey, and then the car had exploded? Truly, I believe we were protected, for there was much to be done, and the healing of the man's leg was just the proof I needed that all is working out in accordance with a Divine plan. We may never see the hand that guides us, but if we follow our "instincts" we will not go wrong.

How wonderful that, in a country where no words are spoken between patient and healer, the healing takes place — the message is simple. The healer is not the power, simply the instrument, and as long as we realise that and allow ourselves simply to be used for the greater good of those we serve, the Spirit world will use us well.

There are many other such incidents, so more later...

SPIRITUAL SISTERS

For many years I puzzled me as to why, so often, I felt closer to friends than I did to family members. Only when I began to investigate matters of the Spirit, and the energies associated with the people in the Spirit world, and when I further investigated the subtle energies between myself and those around me, did I begin to understand.

As human beings we often feel obliged to "like" our relatives, when sometimes we don't like them at all. We also feel we should love our family members more than we love anyone else. BUT WHAT IF WE DON'T? Does that make us wicked, nasty people?

For many years I thought it did, and so often I felt that I was wicked, but more and more during the past 18 years I have come to know that ties of blood do not equate with ties of a Spiritual nature. In other words we can feel totally alien in our blood family, and yet feel totally at home, and at peace, with people we have known a very short while.

Due to this understanding I have an incredibly extended family, which reaches to many corners of this world. Indeed I am constantly surprised by how many people, who I've met through my work for and with the Spirit world, have taken me to their hearts, and have included me in their plans for family gatherings.

This has been a source of great joy to me, especially as I have had so many disappointments in my own private life.

Muriel, of whom you will read much throughout this book, was someone I became close to when we were both married, and involved with Fleetwood Sea Cadets — our lives certainly took a very different turn when we became involved with Spiritualism. We have retained a friendship for 22 years now, a friendship which has survived many stressful, traumatic conditions on both sides. We learnt long ago that we must just "be there" for each other when there is a need. Our personalities are totally different, and yet funnily enough, we have come to look more like each other, especially during the past five years (a little like dogs and masters perhaps?).

During the early days of my mediumship it was Muriel who came to each church service or demonstration when it was my first time at a venue, Muriel who offered constructive criticism, Muriel who was circle leader when we had a circle in someone's home at St. Annes, and Muriel who was my absolute confidante. There are not many people in life to whom we can truly confide our innermost fears, joys hopes and dreams are there? For me Muriel was that person, and I hope I have been there for her, when she needed me the most.

Lotte was another person with whom I established a true rapport, someone else in whom I could confide, who never judged, but would offer helpful advice, and lots of tender loving care. Lotte and I discussed family matters in great detail, matters of the Spirit in great depth, and when possible, we indulged in something we called "finger walking". I must offer a word of caution here, before I explain finger walking. The use of a ouija board is not something to be taken lightly, nor should it be used by anyone who is under the influence of drink or drugs, or anyone who is mentally unstable.

A long time ago I was encouraged by my voice to approach this means of communication in a very organised and disciplined way. indeed I was taught properly how to approach Spirit using a glass and the letters of the alphabet.

Whenever I stayed with Lotte, we would take the opportunity of "finger walking" at least once each visit. She loved it so much, and not just for the "messages" from loved ones. Many times we received simple philosophy, with proof of who was giving it to us, and never did we receive any information which could be detrimental.

I remember well that last visit to Lotte and Ernie, when I said to her "On Friday let us do finger walking for the last time". Little did I realise that it actually would be the last time EVER that we would sit with Spirit in this way.

Whenever I stayed with Ernie and Lotte I could drop the public facade, could sleep when I needed, rest when I wanted, in fact their home was my home whenever I visited — lovely.

During a period of time Lotte and I became so close that whenever we were out people asked if we were sisters, as they do when Muriel and I are together. Now, the questions are asked so often it is just easier to say "Yes" than to explain our friendship.

Another of my spiritual "sisters" is Ursula. Ursula and I met around 14 years ago, when I went to Blackburn Spiritualist Church. At that time we had no more contact than just passing the time of day with each other prior to the church service.

It was in 1987 that we first socialised, and in 1988 that we really began a friendship that has become incredibly close. Although Ursula is some years older than I am, it has also come to my attention, many times, that physical age means nothing at all. All of my friends throughout my adult life have been older than me, some as many as 25 years.

Ursula's life changed dramatically about 12 months after my marriage broke up, and we somehow got into the habit of socialising whenever I visited the church. Then one Christmas I should have been going to America but at the last minute couldn't go. Ursula invited me to spend Christmas with her family, and that has set the scene for my Christmases ever since, apart from a couple that I did actually spend in America.

So what DOES make us feel so close to people who are not related to us by birth?

Is it the bond of friendship because we are so alike? Certainly not in the case of Muriel and I.

Is it because of cultural similarities? Certainly not in the case of Lotte and I — Lotte was Danish, and I'm English.

Is it because of age and background? Certainly not in the case of Ursula and I — Ursula is 20 years older and German — she only came to England in her 30s.

So, we must ask ourselves, what DOES bring us together, in a way and with a knowledge that suggests we know each other in the deepest sense possible? I have come to the conclusion that it is the same need for Spiritual truth, understanding and knowledge, the same type of curious minds that are not satisfied simply to be told what to think — but minds that must KNOW for themselves. All of the people I feel closest to are explorers, investigators, people who use much time and energy in finding out the greater meaning of life, wanting to understand the Spiritual purpose behind everything, not just for personal understanding, but because to know there is greater reason than just existing for the customary three score years and ten encourages each one of us to find a means of furthering our spiritual growth.

What I find wonderful is that when so many people of like minds come together, no matter the age, culture or past religious knowledge, there is a true feeling of family is established very quickly.

My dream is to bring together all the people I love, as family, together in one venue.

THE FEBRUARY FAMILY GATHERING

To some degree I experience that each February, when people come from far and wide to a seminar, which it is my joy and privilege to organise each year.

I started this some years ago, for reasons already explained, and I can truly say this has become the highlight of my year.

In my capacity as organiser I bring together a team of mediums and speakers who will enjoy working with each other, and who will complement each other, in every sense of the word.

The programme is arranged in such a way that there is truly something for everybody, with lectures, Tai Chi and meditation classes throughout the day, and social evenings after the day's events.

At each seminar there are at least six working mediums who have booked in for a break, and to refresh their Spiritual selves, knowing that they can simply be one of the crowd instead of being expected to "perform". Mediumship is not a performance — it is a sacred trust. Mediums are not performers, they are merely the eyes and ears of the Spirit world, and as such they need not always be "on duty".

My greatest joy is to see newcomers arrive at the hotel where we hold the seminars, to see their shyness, and yet to know that within half of an hour of their being there, someone who has been coming for years will quickly include them in a conversation, regulars wishing to establish a true feeling of family.

In the past I attended so many seminars, and at other venues around the country, and so many times I felt there was not a truly welcoming attitude, except whenever I attended one of the Lynwood Fellowship seminars. Indeed, working for Lynwood, and attending the seminars organised by Don Galloway, taught me so much about how important a welcome is. I will always be grateful to Don, and the wonderful people I met through Lynwood, because at a very difficult time in my life, emotionally as well as Spiritually, the love of Lynwood wrapped itself around me, making me feel safe. Through them I found Spiritual fathers, mothers, brothers and sisters, some of whom are now in the Spirit world, but all have a special place in my heart.

SEMINARS = SPIRITUAL REFRESHMENT

Every time I organise a seminar someone asks if they are simply for mediums — in other words are they for people who already know the direction their Spiritual gifts should take them?

It is difficult to explain, in words, that we all have gifts of the Spirit. At the seminars we very quickly realise that we DO all have gifts, and that not everyone else knows more than we do. Such a revelation allows the individual to relax a little, and to enjoy the processes of unfoldment, as well as the means of getting to know the other people who are attending the various courses.

Here again like attracts like, although when we first come together and begin to explore ideas together we often find we approach the other people through the physical senses.

In other words we judge a lot by what we see — a big mistake, but a common one, and one which when discovered to be a mistake often creates some laughter and certainly breaks any tensions.

Perfectly made up, beautifully manicured, everything physically as it should be. She couldn't possibly have any problems could she?

Well could she?

Oh yes, indeed she could. She may not be there for the same reasons as most of the people attending, but because she has suffered dreadfully through losing some of her nearest and dearest relatives, she just doesn't show her feelings to the world.

The newly developing medium would look with physical eyes, whilst the sensitive medium will FEEL with her Spiritual senses and will, in gentle and loving ways, find a means of breaking down the barrier of privacy created by the woman.

It is quite amazing the difference in the type of people who attend seminars. People from all different material backgrounds. Some have saved each week just to attend one week's seminar whilst others have no financial problems in paying at all. We have doctors, barristers, people from the medical profession, as well as people from complementary medicines, builders, plumbers, artists, in fact people from all walks of life.

Remember we are split personalities, to the extent that we are Spirit confined in a human body, and therefore we are all the same under the skin. If we were all given an identical outfit, and put in the middle of a field to get to know each other, what would we do? There would be no point simply looking at the other people would there, for we would merely see a physical mirror image? Therefore, if we could learn to ignore the physical senses and develop more Spiritual understanding we would truly learn to know our fellow man.

During the years I have been organising seminars I have been amazed by the loving qualities of those people I have associated with. On my seminars we have truly proven that love breeds love, and positive thought breeds positive outlook. This, in turn, follows through into the lives of those who have attended when they leave, which is why so many people come back year after year. No matter the type of work you do, no matter how important the position you hold in the world, in the company you work for, or the business you own, you are YOU — and YOU need some time, sometimes simply to BE. I can only pray that when you do give yourself time you will find a loving group of people such as those who attend my seminars, and that you will feel at home with them and dare to be yourself.

TEN MOST FREQUENTLY ASKED QUESTIONS

After every demonstration, during workshops, and as part of discussions and question and answer sessions, I have found that the same questions crop up, time and time again.

During the early days of learning to understand my gifts I found I had so many questions, but sadly I could not find people who were willing to help me to find the answers. Therefore, I devised a means of finding out for myself — each night, for half an hour, I set aside time for a meditation with a difference. I would sit quietly, pen and paper at hand, and would pose questions, to which I would frequently be given the answers.

Realising the frustration of needing to KNOW I thought it may be helpful to you to have the answers to the questions that most people ask. However, do remember that every answer will raise in you more questions (I hope). No one person has all the answers and I am merely offering you the answers in accordance with my experience.

1.   WHEN DID YOU FIRST KNOW YOU WERE A MEDIUM?

According to my mother I spoke with an "imaginary friend" as if she was real, to such an extent that my mother would lay a place at the table, and should anyone sit next to me on the bus I would scream that they had sat on my "friend".

Sadly for me, my "friend" left me when my sister was born, when I was four and a half years of age. My first memory of a Spirit communicator is of coming home from school, at the age of about eight, and hearing a voice in my head — the voice of a little girl but not my own voice.

No matter where I went, or how I tried to get rid of her, she wouldn't go. I did not dare tell anyone because they may say I was mad. I had heard of people being locked away for such imaginings.

I can remember, aged nine, coming home from school along Broadway in Fleetwood, and every day the girl's voice would count the cracks in the paving slabs. Aha, I thought, I'll fool her — I'll go another way. Well, of course that didn't work, for when voices talk to you they are practising a form of telepathy, and even though you cannot see the owner of the voice, you know it is real.

Occasionally I slipped up, and would say some of the things that my voice impressed me to say. For example I remember telling a friend of my mother "I don't know why you come to see my mum— she doesn't like you very much". (I remember it well because of the smack I received — this was the start of my learning NOT to speak of the truths that my inner voices spoke to me — self preservation was very high on my list of priorities at that stage).

How was I to know that as I was speaking I was merely repeating my mother's thoughts?

I had a one-sided argument with the voice, the first of many such arguments, or rather I should say, times of my laying down the law and being ignored.

The voices continued and I tried simply to put them to one side, and it seemed to work, but the message will always get through, no matter how hard you try to ignore the voices. You cannot stop yourself thinking, can you, and therefore it became a challenge to those in Spirit to impress my mind without making me aware of an actual voice — and this they did until I consciously decided to investigate the whole business some 25 years later.

2. DOESN'T YOUR CONTACT WITH SPIRIT FRIGHTEN YOU?

The only fear is fear itself, or so we are told. However, what we do always seem to fear is the unknown, don't you think? Therefore, if we investigate and establish a truth there can be nothing to fear.

My stock answer to this question is "No, I'm more afraid of walking past a pub, at closing time, when the drunks are coming out". This is not a glib response — it is a genuine heartfelt truth.

People, I find, are people — no matter whether they are of this physical world, or if they are in the Spirit world, and what I work with are the personalities of those people who have merely passed to Spirit. Why, then, should I fear them?

It IS important to establish the nature of the people you are linking with, and never assume that every voice you hear, or every Spirit person you see, is good.

If we have positive and negative energy here wouldn't it seem natural to have the same in the Spirit world. We don't become saints when we pass to Spirit — we merely leave behind the physical body, yet retaining that which we have become — truly a time to reap what we have sown. Therefore, if your father was so insecure that he flew into jealous rages, it would follow that a minute after he passed to Spirit he would be exactly the same. It would be up to him to wish to progress, and then help would be given, and he may communicate, through a medium, the way he was for recognition, but could then explain his new thoughts and feelings.

Many people contact me because they have had private sittings with "mediums" without them having any understanding of mediumship. As in every other aspect of life there are varying levels of mediumship, for the quality of the contact is dependent upon the development of the medium.

All too often people are given messages, purported to have come from loved ones, yet which have left them feeling worried, sad or afraid.

Let me give you an example.

Some years ago I visited a home in Fleetwood to do some private sittings. All the ladies were nervous and edgy, and after the second one I asked what on earth was the matter with them.

I was told they had visited a local psychic a few weeks previously, who had given each one of them a message, the content of which had truly frightened them.

I asked if she had established <u>who</u> was communicating the information to the "medium" and after a long discussion we found that at no time did she establish WHO was giving the communications. The first rule of mediumship is that before giving any message, you should establish from whom the message is coming.

For example — if I gave you proof that your grandmother was communicating a message, proof that you accepted, and if she had been a lovely, protective type of grandmother, then it would be natural that you could accept the message she gave.

On the other hand, if you were merely offered a lot of words, with no knowledge of who the communicator was, why would you accept anything that was said. Would you take advice from a stranger in the street? No, of course not, and whilst I realise that many psychics have a type of hypnotic energy when you are in their presence, that energy wanes immediately you leave them.

The reverse of this is when you visit a medium who establishes contact with a loved one, gives you a message from them, establishing that communication really is taking place. When you leave the FEELING of having been in the presence of someone who cared about your welfare remains with you, sometimes for weeks to come.

Please do use your common sense when visiting psychics and mediums. None of us have all the answers — we only have knowledge to the extent of our own experiences, and mediums ARE people, so please don't give us the right to direct your lives. If you approach mediumship with an open mind, apply lots of common sense and analyse everything, you will never be frightened of Spirit.

3.   WHY DO THEY COME BACK WITH THE AILMENTS THEY PASSED WITH?

For those of us who are privileged to be the link between you and your loved ones, there must be a means of passing on as quickly as possible who the communicator is. This establishes the credibility of the medium, doesn't it?

Therefore, if you nursed your mother through lung cancer, to her death, the emotional memory of that will remain with you, and if she can find no other means of communicating who she is, your mother will momentarily give the medium the feeling of the condition which was the cause of her death.

Of course, your loved ones have none of the physical or mental disabilities they had when on the earth — physical ailments belong to the physical body. The soul has journeyed on, and has an awareness of the physical world without any of the baggage we carry through this life.

The Spirit people will always find the easiest way to establish who they are, and much depends, on the medium's abilities. So, if a medium SENSES the Spirit people, she will sense the pain and the suffering, but once that is established she will feel it no more and will be able to pass on the communication.

At a later date it may help you to know a little more about how mediumship actually functions, but for now, I must continue with the answers to the questions.

4.   WHAT HAPPENS TO PEOPLE WHO COMMIT SUICIDE — ARE THEY PUNISHED?

There seems to be no greater sorrow than that of someone whose loved one has taken his or her own life. Sadly, the grieving process often cannot be completed because those left behind have so many unanswered questions, and the only person who has the answers is no longer with them.

Guilt is the most difficult thing to come to terms with, and even if there should be no guilt attached to anyone, grief can not be rationalised.

To the critics who say that mediumship harms people I would say, talk to someone whose loved one committed suicide, and who then received evidence from a medium of the survival of that loved one, after death. Ask them if the reassurances received have helped them comes to terms with their loss. If those who criticise and doubt can offer the same level of proof and subsequent acceptance that they need to feel no guilt, but should be content to get on with their life, then let them prove it.

Meantime, let those of us who work with the love of the Spirit, hoping each time we work to give comfort and consolation to those who are sad, get on with it.

The greatest joy, for me personally, is when someone in Spirit, at the end of a sitting or public message, thanks me for having given their message in such a way that they can now seek their progress, knowing their loved ones will be able to get on with their lives, and in time, will remember only the happy times. Of course there is no punishment — it is usually established that it was merely their time to pass on and help was waiting for them.

5. I HAVE BEEN MARRIED MORE THAN ONCE — WHO WILL I BE WITH WHEN I DIE?

Marriage is a state of being created by man — true marriage is a bonding and blending of souls. Are you happily married, do you want to spend eternity with the person you are now with, or do you merely exist wishing you were with someone else?

So many of the questions I am asked actually require little more than common sense. Everyone knows what they want and what they need, and whilst many times other issues come into our lives to confuse us, the true knowledge is within us, if we would only take time to discover it. All too often, people come to mediums hoping to "pass the buck" — in other words they are afraid of making the decisions on their own, for then they would have to be responsible for the outcome of each situation.

Emotion belongs to the physical world, to the extent that emotion often clouds common sense, and therefore, it seems quite logical to assume that when we pass we are able to see things more clearly.

Look around your life now, and the people in it — if you were told this very minute that you will die in 30 seconds, how many of those people could you happily live with for ever and ever?

My belief is that, when in the Spirit world, you will be with whoever you are soul bonded with. It may be the children/spouse, friends you have lived most closely with in this life, or it may be someone who you felt incredibly close to, but they passed right through your life very quickly.

I remember one lady asking that very question, quite seriously, at the end of her message in a public demonstration. Her response to my answer had everyone in fits of laughter when she said she had had five husbands, and had loved them all the same. "In that case," I said, "you will probably be with them all in the Spirit world."

This is one of those things that cannot be proven, so use your own judgement believe what you feel to be right, until the time you pass, then you will KNOW the truth.

6.   I DIDN'T HAVE TIME TO SAY GOODBYE — DID MY LOVED ONE KNOW THAT I LOVED THEM, AND WILL YOU TELL THEM THAT I STILL DO?

The questions you need answers to are known by your loved ones who are now in Spirit, and when the time is right, and your loved ones choose the time, I can assure you the answers will come!

In other words you may book to have a sitting with a medium, or suddenly turn up at a public demonstration or church service, and the answers to your questions will be given without the medium knowing anything about you.

This particular question is asked, either mentally or verbally, by a large proportion of people seeking knowledge of life after death.

Imagine for a moment that you have nursed your partner for months, been awake night after night, tended to their physical needs, fed them, and done everything possible for them. Two minutes before they pass the nurse who has been brought in suggests you go to get yourself a cup of tea, or have a little walk round, and the minute you leave the room they pass to Spirit. How do you think you would feel?

This is something that has happened to countless hundreds of people, many of them feeling so guilty they cannot rebuild their lives.

Your partner, now in the Spirit world, knowing how you feel, will try any means possible to let you know that it was the right time for him/her to pass — and frequently they say that it was easier for them to pass knowing you were NOT watching for the precise moment. Think, for a minute, of a time when you have to go to an airport or railway station to say goodbye to someone you may never see again, and remember the emotion then. This is only a fraction of the emotion that affects us when we KNOW that someone is about to pass and we wonder how we will cope with the actual moment of their passing.

The time of physical death actually belongs entirely to the person who is about to go, so should it not be considered that they are the ones whose feelings should be taken into account, rather than the people who are waiting to say goodbye.

Physically, we are incredibly resilient. Throughout our lives there are so many times we must pick up the pieces after times of trauma and sadness. When we are tiny and a grandparent dies. When we are teenagers and that first love affair breaks up. When we are young adults and suffer a failed marriage. When we are looking forward to being parents but lose the baby. When we are hoping for a long and happy marriage and a partner passes to Spirit suddenly at a young age.

Why then, after dealing with so many of these problems, do we find it so necessary to know if our loved one, newly passed, knew how much we loved them? BECAUSE IT IS OUR NEED TO DO SO.

Part of the grieving process is the "poor me" feeling. Whilst we know our loved ones are safely on the other side, that they cannot suffer any more, WE are the ones left behind with our grief, and so every thought and feeling will centre around what we need to know.

Mediumship performs its greatest service to those who feel so heartbroken they cannot carry on living, particularly in cases when there were things not spoken about between the person who has passed and the one left behind.

Sometimes, at the end of a sitting, during which contact has been established for the recipient by their nearest and dearest, the sitter will say "Will you tell my husband I loved him, and I always will". I find this quite an emotional moment, no matter how often it is said, but I always say that he knows, as he did in life.

Many of us were brought up not to express in words how we feel about someone else, and so by deeds we prove our love. So many couples seem to take each other for granted, but in fact that is the essence of trust placed in each other, with no need for words. Let that thought comfort those of you who did not have the opportunity to say goodbye, and when your still, inner voice suggests to you that your loved one can still communicate his feelings, know it is not imagination, but a remembrance of the physical contact you had, now taken to a deeper level of understanding.

7.   CAN YOU GET IN TOUCH WITH A SPECIFIC PERSON?

I was once told that there was a medium, some years ago, of whom you could ask such a question, and he would furnish you with proof of that particular loved one's presence. However, in my experience it is better NOT to ask for a specific person to communicate with you.

Imagine you had a son, who recently died in a road accident, and you go along to a medium who knows nothing about you at all, and during the course of the message you receive your son establishes his personality, tells you lots of little personal things known only to you, and convinces you that he is OK and that he is happy for you just to get on with your life knowing he will watch over you.

If this is all you need or ever will need to re-establish your normal routine of life, happily, then of course there is no need for you to investigate further.

BUT, in most cases, the grieving process is such that it takes a very long time for people to come to terms with loss, particularly when that loss is of their child, or children.

During the early stages of grieving, if you investigate matters pertaining to life after death, it is often considered by those in Spirit that you should be given snippets of information, like individual pieces of a jigsaw, pieces that may relate to the past and present, but often giving you a bit of information about something that is yet to happen, and which will be proven at a later date.

When you are told of something that will happen that does actually come true, does not that make you think more deeply about the source of the information, especially when the personality of your son was established, by the medium, and he was the one giving you the message?

Doesn't that make you think there really is an intelligence behind the information, and doesn't that make you realise that your son is not dead?

Having thought all this through, wouldn't it activate within you a need to know more and more, thus giving your son the opportunity to further prove his continuing existence, this giving credence to the fact that life after death can be and is established so often?

May I suggest then that those people in the Spirit world know of our real needs, and will always do their best to help us to find our individual truths in the best way for each one of us. Your needs are not mine, and mine are not the same as yours, and so let us leave to those in Spirit the right to know when the time, place and medium are the right ones for their need to prove they have survived death.

8.   HOW DO I KNOW IF I HAVE SPIRITUAL GIFTS AND HOW DO I DEVELOP THEM?

This question could take so long to answer that it would need a whole book to deal with the enormity of the question.

Firstly, let me assure you we ALL have Spiritual gifts. Whilst people sometimes try to convince us that they are more clever, more beautiful and more knowledgeable than we, if we would stop comparing ourselves to other people, and concentrate on that which we are and that which we have, we could understand the direction in which our gifts should be taking us.

Thoughts to ponder on (Questions)
(a) Have you ever had a sudden urge to telephone someone you haven't seen for a long time, and was their response to say how much they needed help at that time?

(b) Or did you, for no apparent reason, think of someone you have had no contact with, and a letter from them arrived, totally out of the blue?

(c) Do you sometimes KNOW without being told of the pain of another person, whether that pain is emotional or physical?

(d) Are you the sort of person everyone tells their troubles and woes to, and do you find it easy to respect their confidence, keeping it entirely to yourself?

(e) Do answers to people's questions come directly to your mind, even though you have no personal experience of the situation they are needing advice about, and do they then thank you for your response, which has offered them some enlightenment?

Suggested Spiritual Gifts (Answers)

(a) Precognition, which is the ability to receive knowledge of something which is yet to take place. Many people have such a gift, often related to world happenings or, mothers who are particularly well bonded with their children have such a gift, and will always test it.

(b) Depends on how you receive the thought — as a voice could suggest the gift of clairaudience (the ability to hear Spirit), or if you mentally see the person who has written the letter you could have the gift of clairvoyance (the ability to see clearly). Usually associated with people, who become good Spiritual healers, who not only feel other people's pains, but have a genuine desire to help when possible (good nurses and doctors who incorporate genuine feeling and caring for their patients are natural healers).

(c) Also, the gift of healing, but can manifest differently — instead of healing by laying on hands, you may find you are better suited to acting as a listener and advisor.

(d) Again, more suited to counselling, but be careful not to take on the role of playing at being "God". Know that if you offer advice, that advice may be taken and therefore it is up to you, in times when you do not have all the answers, to refer the person to someone who can help them more than you can.

(e) Obviously mediumistic, and needing to know the mechanics of your mediumship through practice, usually by approaching other people, such as mediums, and others who have travelled the path before you, to encourage their Spiritual gifts.

Do remember that each medium only has knowledge in accordance with their own experiences, and in accordance with Divine Law, which incorporates the teachings he/she receives from helpers in the Spirit world.

You can be guided but no-one can give you your Spiritual gifts, for you ARE your own gifts.

No-one can teach you, but they can encourage you to unfold naturally — the knowledge is within you, so be careful not to give anyone else the right to direct your Spiritual gifts, but rather seek help and guidance, and then decide for yourself what feels right.

9. WHY DOES GOD TAKE CHILDREN FROM US?

I can honestly say that in all the years I have worked with Spirit, nothing has touched me as much as my links with parents whose children have passed to the Spirit world. There is nothing normal about such a happening — children should survive their parents, shouldn't they?

How do parents cope after the death of their children? What sense can they make of the reason for the death? And how hurt do they feel when they believe that God has punished them, for some strange reason, by taking their child away from them?

There are so many questions that I could give you 101 examples of how, through my mediumship, I have been able to re-unite children and parents. However, I do not feel this is the right time. I am sure you will agree that children bring a beauty and a love into our lives that is unequalled — they truly are a blessing, and if they are well and happy that is a bonus. Those of us who have happy, healthy children take that for granted, because we don't know anything different — parents who have children who are sick from birth know the difference (unless they have had other healthy children).

One of the most remarkable situations I ever witnessed was at a hospital for terminally ill children. A young friend of mine was terminally ill with cancer, and he was recuperating there after yet another operation. He truly was an amazing young man — at the age of 11 he had more wisdom than most of us will achieve in a whole lifetime.

I went to visit him, and took stock of the way parents were allowed to nurse their children, to feed them, to bathe them — in fact doing all the normal things that parents do for children, but sadly in a very unnatural situation.

What I saw was that the children had become the teachers, and the parents the pupils of life.

The children reassured the parents, even the very young ones, not demanding as children do quite naturally. I wondered if the severity of their illness created something special in them. It seemed the message to be sent from their soul was that a time of preparation was at hand, and that they the patients knew and accepted this, and their current mission was to encourage the grown-ups to believe it, and accept it, also.

What a strange environment to be in, but how privileged I felt to be able to share that atmosphere for a short time, and how grateful I was that I could walk away from there, my life intact.

My little friend did pass to Spirit shortly afterwards. His mum had recently lost her daughter in a car crash, and so now she was without the two children she had loved and worked so hard for.

Her form of therapy was to help the other parents of terminally ill children, but not everyone can react in the same way.

Sometimes parents create shrines to their children, visit graves every day, put flowers by photos every day, talk to photos of their children, and chastise them for no longer being around.

Everything that seems peculiar, or abnormal, to those who are NOT suffering is actually very normal to the parents of children who have passed — their only consolation being that for a short time God bestowed upon them the blessing of a child to love.

You see God is not cruel. He does not wilfully take from us those we love — he actually GIVES us something very special, and if you are one of those parents who have lost a child I hope you will remember them with joy, and that that will remove some of your pain. Nothing I, or anyone else, can say can help — especially as I have not the same experience, but there are organisations which can help.

10.   ARE YOU AFRAID OF DYING?

I used to think that this was a strange question, and would react quite sharply by saying of course not, but actually the question itself is much larger than it at first appears.

To the basic question, I have no fear of dying, but I am concerned about the manner of my death. Wouldn't it be wonderful if we knew how and when we were going to die? At first thought it would seem to be wonderful, but then we would be fearful of the way we would approach that time, and so, in accordance with Divine Law, we are given no logical knowledge of how and when we will pass.

I use my wording very carefully, because I do believe that the majority of people DO have prior knowledge and react accordingly, but that knowledge may be purely a sensing, not acknowledged by logical mind.

Take, for example, the husband of a friend who, twice a week, took his son to a youth organisation, came home, left his car on the drive, then picked his son up later.

On the day he passed (very suddenly in his early 30s) he took his son as usual, returned home, put his car in the garage, tidied up his belongings in the house and promptly passed to Spirit, with no prior health warnings whatsoever.

Thankfully, due to so many communications from Spirit, I know there is nothing to fear from death. Already, I am living the best way I possibly can because I know I will judge my own life when I pass, and in the meantime my loved ones are watching over me, and I don't want them to feel ashamed of me, do I?

Whilst I often think there is more to fear in life than in death, I have come to appreciate quite recently, due to health problems, that the quality of our lives is the most important thing — death will come when it is ready, and I hope that I, like you, will be ready for it when it does.

At least we KNOW there is no death, that life is eternal, and that our loved ones will be waiting for us. So what is there to fear?

PLATFORM WORK

It is easy, looking back, to see a pattern of life unfolding, but when it is your life, and you are in the midst of it, it is sometimes difficult to see the complete picture, for you are the threads being woven into a tapestry, in a manner of speaking.

The transition from Val Williams, visitor to churches, and someone who would give tiny messages to people in an open circle, to Val Williams, public working professional medium, was not an easy one.

From the outset, in my area, we were told that we should use our "gifts" of mediumship wisely — should not charge money for any of the work we did — and this was something I liked the thought of, never intending to be a professional medium, but just wanting, in some small way, to use my gifts to help other people. In fact I remember saying quite positively at some point "The day I have to do this for a living will be the day I give up". Little did I know in those early days of innocence that many of those people telling we newcomers not to use our gifts for gain were actually doing that themselves, and in fact they were very afraid of what they thought could be "competition". This is something I have never understood, as I believe that if there were a thousand GOOD mediums in one area there still would not be enough. (Good mediums being those people who can receive communication from the Spirit world and convey those messages to sitters and to those seeking truth through our demonstrations).

How well I remember in those early days of innocence feeling terribly guilty the day I took £1 for a sitting I'd done for someone — having done sittings for no money at all for two years because I did not feel my standard of work was good enough. I very quickly learnt about people — and I have had many confirmations of my idea, that those who cannot afford a sitting will save and save until they can afford it, but often people who have money would rather not pay for a sitting, and will say they have no money.

I also found that if I did not charge something, most people would feel obliged to buy a gift, often costing more than a sitting would be, and sometimes more than they could afford, so a nominal fee was set.

Had I then come into the realms of professional mediums — something I had always said I would not do? The reason for this was simple — in the December my then husband had come home and said his firm had gone bankrupt overnight, and there was no money for wages, holiday pay or anything else, no money at all, and this just three weeks before Christmas.

A couple of weeks earlier, having already bought our Christmas food, I had provided a meal for some American visitors who had been kind to us when we had visited New York. So here we were with no food, no money, no present for our young son — what a frightening time.

Instead of panicking as I had done on an earlier occasion, I merely went upstairs, sat on the bed and said to my voice "Well, you have always said you will provide, and I think now is the time to prove it".

Half an hour later the phone rang, with someone requesting sittings, and from then until my husband got another job some seven months later there was enough each week to pay our bills, though not a penny over. In the July, when he began another job, the phone stopped ringing — just another way of those in the Spirit world proving how much help and loving guidance they are willing to give us.

By this time, also, I was being invited to many churches in the locality to take services, do demonstrations etc, and whilst I was married merely charged the churches my petrol money, the household money providing the means of transport etc.

Therefore I could not be classed as a professional medium, to my great relief. I continued to do private sittings, often going out in the evening to do a group, the money being used to supplement our income, which was very little.

The diary, at that time, was becoming more and more full, and the more I did the more I realised what a responsibility I had taken on, because I had to work harder and harder to understand my mediumistic gifts, to discipline the time I applied to understanding the mechanics of mediumship, and a reverence was certainly applied to our weekly circle — a time I loved more than any other time during the week, and a time which was MY time with the Spirit workers, for they would come lovingly and gently with their messages of inspiration, and I would feel very secure.

To anyone beginning on this pathway of mediumship, I would say — remember that the day you first take a service, or do a demonstration in public, is not the day you end your development for Spirit, but the day you actually begin.

Mediumship is a natural gift, but sometimes the application of the gift is something that needs to be learnt, in a loving, encouraging atmosphere. You need friends to offer constructive criticism and advice, and you need your own point of reference, the inner voice of your guide or helper, and if you combine both worlds you can bring together a great balance in your work for Spirit and the people on earth you will deal with.

I continued working for Spirit in this way, enjoying every moment of the work itself, and of learning to understand HOW it worked, spending any spare time going to seminars, to listen to other mediums' points of view, guidance etc, and then always returning to my inner knowledge to see if I could agree with them. Very quickly I established a rapport with my helpers, and in particular with "my voice", those voices I heard replacing the previously experienced "knowing" that I had always had, ever since I could remember.

I took my first service in 1982, sharing it with Anne Lewis, now in Spirit, but then the President of Cleveleys Church. I owe a great deal to Anne, for she was the first person who recognised my gifts, and who encouraged me to learn more and more.

Having taken the first service I was both hooked and petrified, and so a course of action had to be taken:

a) in order that I should be able to work correctly for Spirit and

b) so that I could gain confidence in my ability to deliver their messages with confidence as well as truth.

To this end I found it vital to analyse every service and demonstration, enjoying the knowledge of the messages which I'd given concisely and evidentially, but also looking for the one message (or more) that I had struggled with, and then maybe had not felt that I had given it absolutely correctly.

Those times of analysis were a great leveller for me, and something I never shirked. I learned the hard way that other people's opinions, whilst interesting, were not necessarily something I agreed with. Therefore it was imperative that I felt that I knew what I needed to do to improve each aspect of my work, from the introduction to the congregation, to the opening prayers, to the talk, and of course the clairvoyance, each stage helping to create that bond with the people attending the demonstrations.

What I really learnt was that it is important to blend the energies of the medium with the energies in the room before beginning to speak, this setting the scene for the Spirit world to manifest in their chosen way, providing the most evidential communications that they, together with the mediums, were capable of.

Platform work, as we call the demonstrations of mediumship that we offer to the public is, to use an overworked phrase, the shop-window, showing to the public as it does the way we work. It is therefore vital that before mediums commence they should KNOW the mechanics of their mediumship. There will always be those of the public who will challenge the knowledge of mediums, who will try to prove that the medium is not being truthful or delivering communications properly, or that messages are fabricated, and so it is not simply a case of being able to deliver the messages.

The task of the public working medium includes the ability to promote the TRUTH of mediumship, which means proving life after death with absolute truth and conviction, not allowing anyone to unsettle the proceedings — not an easy task, and one which can take years to establish but in the words of one of our past prime ministers — "If you put yourself on the firing line you must expect to be shot at" — in other words the minute you are in the public eye, SOMEONE will feel they have a God-given right to challenge you, your work and your truth.

Thankfully, there is a law which protects people from fraudulent mediums, something which was established over 40 years ago, and which protects the rights of the investigators as well as the mediums.

Platform work has provided me with such incredible proof of the true workings of the Spirit world, by surprising me so many times that I could write examples until my last day on this earth, and each time I think they cannot surprise me any more, something else happens to prove me wrong.

During demonstrations it becomes evident how much work goes on in the background, with those from the Spirit world working together to make the contacts they wish to, and by everyone else's loved ones helping with the necessary energy, very much as happens in this world when there is a crisis and everyone rallies around.

To be a part of such energy is uplifting and joyful, and never leaves me feeling tired or drained, and hopefully those attending leave with that same feeling — a feeling that love has touched their lives once again.

My public work has taken me to many countries abroad, and I have found on every occasion that there are no barriers, not of culture, nor of language, for the communications are based on love, and love knows no language.

TESTIMONIALS

"You changed my Life"
The business of knowing that I can trust my voice has led me along a pathway of understanding the other senses I have – the ability to see the Spirit people, and to sense them, as well as to hear them.

There have been many times during demonstrations and private sittings when people have not understood some of the information being given to them, and so naturally they challenged me. I am usually able to furnish further information to substantiate what I have said, as it is the Spirit people who wish to communicate and they're usually willing to offer as much information as possible in order to prove who they are.

Please don't get the idea that the people who visit mediums or visit public demonstrations of mediumship are half-witted people, who have little common sense. They are people like you, people with logical minds, emotional understanding with a common sense that is usually used in abundance.

I have included here some examples of people who have received such evidential information, through my mediumship, that they could no longer doubt that the personalities of their loved ones have survived physical death.

EVIDENCE RECEIVED

There are many ways in which communications are passed from the Spirit world via the medium, but I often feel that it is during a public demonstration that some of the most remarkable evidence is proffered, and accepted, and sometimes, just sometimes, the recipients of such messages are kind enough to tell the medium afterwards how much help the message has been.

One such communication was given, through my mediumship, during a public demonstration which was held at the Lindum Hotel, St. Annes. The recipient of the message in question was there for the first time, and I will allow her to tell you the story in her own words.

TO DOROTHY VIA VAL FROM KEN

"In February 1996 I attended a weekend seminar, at the Lindum Hotel, Lytham, St. Annes, Blackpool.

On our first evening I attended a clairvoyance demonstration with my son and his wife. It was a night I will never forget because I was given such wonderful evidence of my husband's survival, in a way that was so typical of my husband's personality when he was on earth. I must explain that my husband loved to make people laugh, and had a loveable mischievous way of doing this.

Val Williams brought my husband's personality through loud and clear, and was correct when she said Ken and I could read each other's thoughts and didn't need words. Ken also told me, through Val, that there would be a house move within the family that was yet to happen, but that I should go ahead with it and that the arrangements met with his approval. Almost twelve months later what I was told then is about to take place. Val then started to laugh and seemed to be arguing with my Ken that she couldn't say what he had told her, and when he insisted she laughed and told me that Ken said I still had some of his underwear and that I was using his nether garments as dusters, as they were better than the dusters you could buy.

The audience erupted into laugher and I felt my face getting redder and redder, and at first I couldn't speak as I was just mortified that he had told the whole room what I knew to be absolutely true, and then I laughed, too, because that's exactly the sort of thing my Ken would do to let me know he knew everything I did and that he was always with me. I could just imagine him laughing his head off at having surprised me so publicly.

My Ken has come through many times since, in many ways, but that time was very special because I know my Ken was having as much fun with Val as he was with me, and with her wonderful gift of sensitivity and honesty I was able to feel that, for those few moments, I was sharing a time of laughter, knowledge and love with my husband and the feeling of happiness and comfort is still with me.

Thank you Val from the bottom of my heart and Ken's. God bless you always. Dorothy."

It is important to note, at this stage, that until a couple of hours before the demonstration I had never set eyes on Dorothy. She was attending my seminar for the very first time, is not a

Spiritualist, but was coming to accompany her son and daughter-in-law, who felt the atmosphere could be very good for her. She has, since that time, attended each and every seminar I have organised at the Lindum Hotel, and she is still finding comfort and joy in her communications, but more than that she is happy to discuss them with other people, particularly those who are a little unsure of what mediumship means.

Another such evidential message was one I was privileged to give to a young lady during an ordinary church service at Otley Spiritualist Church, and again I allow the recipient of the message, in her own words, to explain.

"Dear Val,
I just had to write and thank you for the wonderful message you gave me last Sunday night. (I'm the lady who cried on your shoulder).

You see my mam died 14 years ago today. She drowned herself in the River Don, and had been trying to get a message to me for a long time, because I had always been unsure.

Anyway, it was the first time ever that my mam and dad had come through together. You gave me the answers to some very important questions that only they could answer because I had never asked them. Most of all I want to thank you from the bottom of my heart for the intense love and feeling of inner peace I got from your contact with them. I will now carry that love with me every day of my life.

If I ever had any doubt, you gave me concrete proof that we survive physical death.

I hope you don't mind me writing to you, but there had been so much unhappiness in my life, you gave me a reason to go on with life. I am eternally grateful to you, and I hope that one day I can help someone who is suffering as much as you helped me. Then my life here will not have been wasted. I hope this letter makes some sort of sense to you, once again thank you from the bottom of my heart. God bless you, and may the Spirits keep you safe.

You are a wonderful medium and I will treasure that moment in church for as long as my life continues."

THE INDIVIDUALITY OF TRUTHS ESTABLISHED

I have many other such testimonies, and I include them simply so you can judge for yourself the helpful qualities of mediumship, the reassurances that are evident through both these letters, the first one being from a lady who had not chosen to investigate mediumship before, but when she did it was obvious her husband wanted to re-establish contact with her, as soon, and as evidentially as possible. Interesting to note how he chose to establish his proof. That is something, as mediums, we have no control over — the Spirit people choose their proof — we merely pass it on. Sometimes, to those listening in who are not receiving a message, the messages seem banal, sometimes downright foolish, but the evidential content is something only the recipient can judge. Not for us are what the Americans call "generic" messages, those things that can mean something to everyone, but actual facts that can be understood by those in receipt of the messages — that is how true evidence of communication from the other side of death is established.

The second communication was very different:

Here we have the case of a distraught daughter, wondering why her mother committed suicide, wondering if she could have done more, and wishing to know if her mother was now at peace.

In her own way her mother answered all questions, even choosing the very day of the anniversary of her death to re-establish communication with her daughter in such a way as to fully re-establish peace within her, for now her daughter knew she was re-united in Spirit with her husband, and therefore she was at peace. This, in turn, allowed the daughter to feel more peace than she had felt for the 14 years she had grieved for her sad mother, and so now each one of them, in their own way, and in their own environment, could simply get on with their lives, having had something very special of Spiritual knowledge added to those lives.

I have seen the daughter since, at a recent church service at Otley, and she came to me and told me how much the evidence had helped her long-term, and hopefully it will continue to do so.

There cannot be many more sad circumstances than when someone commits suicide, for no matter their reason, those left behind often feel guilt, anger, frustration, sadness. Indeed every possible emotion of a negative nature, and yet how often have I been privileged to act as a link between someone in the Spirit world and someone on earth who needed to make peace with each other. Never, at any time, have I been told that the person who committed suicide had been punished in any way for that act. Indeed, there have always been ways shown of proving that it was the very right minute when death would have occurred in natural ways, and that, in itself has offered comfort and peace to those left behind. Note what I have said — not empty words of comfort, but words offering PROOF to support the knowledge that it was the right time for the person's life to physically end.

It is not for any one of us to carry the burden of another's life. We come into this world as individuals, and we are brought into contact with many people whose lives we will affect, and whose lives will affect us, whether they be family or friends, but we will go out of this life alone, and so there are many choices en route as to how much we interact with people.

Sometimes, to let those we love know that we are supporting their actions, even if we do not fully understand the reasoning behind those actions, is to offer the greatest love in the world, and so to extend that offering to those in the Spirit world, who have been given an opportunity to end their lives, in their chosen way, knowing it is the true time for their life on earth to end, is truly to offer love in every sense of the word.

If you are still battling to understand why someone you loved chose to end their life, I can only hope that you will think clearly about what I suggest, and should you need further help, I hope you will be able to reach out and seek understanding from someone who has suffered similar tragedy and sadness.

As a medium I can sympathise in such a situation, but I cannot fully understand how you feel, for I have, thankfully, not experienced it on a personal level. Quite often I find myself in a position of being able to put people into contact with each other, for sometimes the mere act of confiding in someone who has understanding of your situation can bring about the start of a healing process. Loneliness can be a terrible thing to bear — but truly there is no need for anyone to be alone in their sadness, and remember, the act of reaching out allows someone else the ability to give where there is need.

We need each other, and we must not be afraid to say so.

Many of the communications I have given have not remained in my conscious memory at all, and one such evidential message was, apparently, given when I visited Glasgow in 1989. Here I offer you the contents of a letter sent to my home after that visit, from a mum whose son had committed suicide three weeks earlier:

"Dear Dear Friend,

I do apologise because I cannot even remember your name. I'm so ashamed about that, because you have made me so unbelievably happy.

I'm the lady who on Monday night you spoke to — my young son committed suicide three weeks ago — he just had too many disappointments in his short life. He was just twenty one last November. As you said our family are all very close and the love we have has been so strong it has helped us all to bear this tragedy. I was so close to John (name changed) and he did always tell me he would step in front of a train if he felt he'd had enough and go on to better things.

This was what he did. He lived in the fast lane and enjoyed his life to the full when he was here. But he never did settle to any one job. He joined the army and that was the happiest job. Sadly he had an accident and was medically discharged. That I think, made him want to go, and he was never scared of dying.

I cannot thank you enough for the joy and the peace of mind you have given me. Now I know he is his own "cheeky carefree self" and I know where he is now and the very strong love we have (all of us) is not broken. We all lived together, Mum, Dad, my sister, my crippled Aunt, myself and John, when he was home.

John also said for me and Arthur (name changed) the man I was with to buy a wee flat for ourselves — now we have and that's what he told us — GO FOR IT.

Thank you, thank you so very very much — and God Bless you — please leave your name at Berkley Street — you'll always be in my heart. Yours thankfully again (name withheld for private reasons)."

We are "told" by those who think they know better, and those people who do not understand mediumship, that mediumship causes hurt to those seeking it. How can this be so when a mother is able to pick up the pieces of her life after losing the love of her life, her son? This letter speaks for itself. I never met the lady again which is the reason I've chosen to withhold her name, and have changed the names of her family members. The greatest benefit to be gained from mediumship is often the ability for the recipient of such a communication to be able to simply pick up the pieces of their life and get on with the business of living day to day, knowing within their heart and soul that their loved one is safe.

One of the questions so often asked is, "How long does it take for someone in Spirit to communicate after their death?" A further question is "When a child dies does someone take care of it, if the parents are still living?".

It really does touch my heart deeply whenever I am able, through my mediumship, to re-unite a child from Spirit with his parents who are grieving and not understanding why their lovely child had to pass before them. Something I think about and talk about very often, because there are no set answers. However, the joy I feel when a child from Spirit trusts me enough to pass on his messages usually over-rides the feelings of sadness.

One such incident occurred in 1998 when I was asked by Ursula if I would do a naming service for Amy, her grand-daughter. I was doubly thrilled because I consider Ursula's family to be my own. Amy was born on my birthday and Ursula's twin grand-daughters were to be named at the same time.

On the evening of the naming service, which was to be incorporated within the usual Sunday evening service, I decided to go outside for a breath of fresh air about ten minutes prior to the start of the evening (something I never did, as I have always felt that mediums should spend quiet time, and should not be seen talking to people just before a service in case this is misconstrued when the evidence from Spirit is being given).

As I was just collecting my thoughts and beginning to formulate the service in my mind a young man and young woman approached the church and began to ask me questions about what happened inside, what sort of services were there etc. In fact all the usual questions people ask when they hear the words "Spiritualist, Spiritualism or mediumship". I explained that the following Thursday there would be an evening of clairvoyance, as there was every Thursday, and that that particular evening was the usual format for a Sunday Service, with hymns, prayers, clairvoyance etc, plus on this occasion a Spiritualist Baptism, and that should they feel the need they would be very welcome. I further suggested that if they felt uncomfortable coming into a Spiritualist church for the first time, they may like to sit near the back in case they wanted to leave before the service finished.

I then excused myself, explaining that I had to go in for the start of the service, not even having mentioned that I was the medium who would be taking the service that night.

The evening went ahead — the naming service was lovely as usual, then I did a talk, we had hymns to enhance the atmosphere, blending everyone together, and then it was time for the clairvoyance.

One communication that evening was truly remarkable, as I became aware of a little boy from the Spirit world who told me he had recently passed and gave particular details of his passing etc.

Having established who the recipients were (his parents), I realised that they were the couple I had been talking to outside the church. From their acceptance of the little boy the evidence flowed thick and fast, his personality establishing itself so strongly that, at one point, his mother was heard to say "look she even has his mannerisms".

The little boy, aged nine, had only passed to Spirit 13 weeks earlier, leaving his parents not only very sad but totally bewildered as well.

Ian made contact initially with his mother, proving himself by mentioning many aspects of his personality, each fact being accepted. He spoke in detail of people living to whom he wished to send his love, and then astounded everyone by two particular pieces of evidence.

a. That a tiny teddy bear was placed in his coffin.

b. He mentioned Tottenham Hotspur, which made his mother gasp as Ian was wearing Tottenham Hotspur shorts on the day he died. Not to be expected in a town where Blackburn Rovers are THE team most people support.

He further talked of a picture which had fallen off the wall. His mother said it was "Footprints" — and that that was true.

Ian's parents were overjoyed to know their little boy had survived death, and I quote "we only wanted to know Ian was alright and now I KNOW he is" said the little boy's parents.

The next time I took a demonstration at the church they were there, and they took the time and trouble to thank me, saying they were able to get on with their lives for they had received the comfort of knowing he was alright.

That evening gave many people many reasons to analyse the workings of Spirit:

The whole evening was geared to children, with it also being a naming service for three little girls. Many parents were in the church, people like Ian's mother and father, and so as the message from Ian was being communicated many others in the room could understand his parents suffering.

Two of the young men from Ursula's family group were astounded apparently, saying afterwards that they could not understand how I was just the Val they had always known until I began to communicate with Spirit and pass on their messages, and particularly when Ian was communicating because they felt I WAS Ian, due to the way his personality established itself.

If mediums are able to establish that the personality of the person in Spirit has survived, how can there be so much doubt about the reality of life after death?

Every day of my life I communicate in some way with YOUR loved ones, and each day of my life it is established in one way or another that death is not the end — it truly is just a stepping stone between the two worlds.

The last testimonial I am including in this chapter, for the purpose of helping you understand how mediumship functions, especially where I have had no prior knowledge of the person I am giving a message to, is one which was sent to me after a lady from America, who I have never met or spoken with, sent me a photo of herself and asked for a postal reading.

This is not as easy to do, as there is no feedback which helps to strengthen the contact, but from an evidential point of view there can be no question.

In such instances I sit quietly, ask Spirit to help, and then record whatever they give to me for the recipient. Below is a portion of the letter sent to me in response to my request for feedback.

Remember I never met the lady, and to this day I have never spoken with her, or been given any information about her from anyone:

"Dear Val,
I hope this note finds you well. I've just been given your new address and it occurred to me that I never did let you know the relevance of the reading you did for me last year.

I listened to my tape several times and decided to type it so that I could read it as well. I am sending a copy to you with notations I made along the way. It was really accurate and right on target in so many areas. It was absolutely wonderful.

Since that time, other revelations that you mentioned have come to pass and others are still unfolding. I am not asking for another reading yet because you stated that whatever is happening in my life, and whatever is going to happen I will see within the next 15 to 20 months. Well, it has been almost 12 months and things in my life are definitely headed in the right direction with every possibility of fitting that time frame exactly. Isn't that so amazing? So, I am waiting, patiently, to see what January brings and finally, May. At that point I am going to write you again and ask for another reading. I am truly happy and not as anxious about tomorrow as I was last year.

Val, thank you so much for my reading. I have listened to my tape and read my copy so many times and it always makes me feel warm on the inside and happy on the outside. Take good care of yourself and I really hope we do get to meet one day.

Fondly (name withheld)."

I have not included any excerpts from her reading, for they are personal — her testimonial is enough to establish for those of you reading, I hope, that mediumship is not mind reading (I had no connection with her mind), nor is it psychological observation (I have not met her and so could not observe her body language).

It is now mid-May so no doubt I shall be hearing from her soon.

These quotes were included hopefully to help make you think. I had no knowledge of the people prior to giving the proof they were to receive. My only source of information being the voices I hear from the world of Spirit. I cannot, of course, expect you to simply believe that there really is a Sprit world unless you have experienced it yourself, any more than I could be expected you to believe that all the people who claim to be mediums can actually receive Spiritual communication. But I can and do suggest you keep an open mind, a sensible point of view, that you neither believe without proof, nor do you totally refuse to accept the possibility of life after death being a reality. I hope that one day you will know that your loved ones have lived on, preferably before you pass to the unseen world!

SPIRITUAL MAGIC

During the summer of 1995/96 I went to Hampshire, to stay with Lotte and Ernie, in readiness for the work I was booked to do at the Portsmouth Temple. As always when time allowed, as Lotte and Ernie were very much part of my extended family, I would try to slot in at least a week, during which we could spend time together in a way that had become quite a routine. There were certain shops I liked to visit, and I always took the opportunity to write my Christmas cards during the time I was there, which on this particular occasion was for two weeks.

During the course of each visit Lotte would drive us somewhere into the country, as she loved to show off the views of the beautiful county in which she lived.

Their grand-daughter Jordan was staying with us at this time, but she was rather unwell, and Lotte felt sure it would do her good to have a nice drive out, and as my car was on the drive I offered to be chauffeur. However, when I tried to start the car it was as dead as a do-do, so after a couple of aborted attempts we rolled my car down the road, got Lotte's out of the garage, intending to call the RAC later, and duly set off for our afternoon out.

What a magical day that turned out to be. We went to town first of all, to run some errands, called at a cafe for a snack, and then, on the way home, Lotte being Lotte, decided to drive through the most beautiful countryside she could find. (She told me later that if I had been driving she would have simply directed me home via the main roads). Imagine our surprise when suddenly, as we turned a corner not one but six beautiful deer came from the left hand side, and one by one seemed to fly right over the bonnet of the car.

It was one of those wonderful moments we talked about for a long time, and how happy we were that my car had broken down!

It was, therefore, of particular surprise and interest to us to find, on our return, that immediately I put the key in the ignition, the car started with no trouble at all!!!

PRAYERS ARE LIVING THINGS

The events of the day did not end there, though, because before we actually arrived home we went down another country lane, approximately ten minutes after Lotte had mentioned that a particular sadness had been felt by everyone in her area recently, when a car containing four people had crashed into a tree, killing three of the occupants.

As we began to drive along yet another country lane Lotte said that the actual tree into which the car had crashed was just ahead, on the left hand side. As we approached it I noticed a young, dark haired man walking away from the tree and coming towards us. Instinctively I knew that this was the survivor of the crash, and I felt the most incredible sadness well up inside me, to such an extent that I wanted Lotte to stop the car so that I could speak to him. How stupid, I thought, I don't know him, what could I have to say that would be of help to him. I mentioned this to Lotte and she, being a truly Spiritually minded person, said she would turn the car around so that I could talk with him, but I said "No" because we had Ernie and little Jordan with us, and it did seem rather a strange thing to want to do.

I have always felt guilty because I did not follow my very strong impression, but my mediumship has functioned in this way since I was born, and unless I am TOLD what to say and why, I tend to feel that I must not intrude into people's lives. It is not the job of a medium to be a nosey-parker psychic.

Looking back now I realise that, in fact, the young man had probably, whilst paying respect to the memory of his friends, prayed very hard for help of some kind, and there we were, possibly able to offer a few words of comfort, or at the very least showing him that prayers are heard.

For a couple of days I could not get the sight of him, and his undoubted sadness, out of my mind, and I said to my Spirit helpers at that stage "If ever there is any way I can help him, please point me in the right direction".

It was some 15 months later that my prayer was answered, in a way that I could not possibly have envisaged, and I will recount now exactly what happened.

In September 1996 I worked for the Lynwood Fellowship at Stansted Hall, and whilst there I met Victor, an osteopath. He had come with a group of friends, and so was introduced to me on the first day. During the week we had many conversations on many levels and I found I enjoyed his company and respected his ideas. I also noticed the Spiritual love he showed to everyone he met, for when he knew they were in pain he immediately did what he could to alleviate that pain, something that I found quite amazing, bearing in mind he is an osteopath, and here he was for a rest period, yet still willing to use his skills to help where and when needed.

At that time I was living in Rotherham, and Victor in Burnley, where he holds his clinic, and when we said our goodbyes on the Saturday morning he said that if I was ever in the area I should be sure to look him up.

The following week I was driving to Portsmouth, again, and was thinking of how Victor could help me with the stiffness in my back. Immediately I arrived at Lotte's I explained that I wanted to find a toning tables studio, which I hoped would loosen my back muscles, which in turn could help Victor to help me.

Lotte gave me the Yellow Pages, and I looked through the listing of places that had toning tables, but as nothing seemed to appeal to me I put the book to one side and had a cup of coffee and a chat. Some ten minutes later I picked up the telephone book again, looked down the lists again, and found one that simply said the name of the Studio, a tiny insignificant advertisement.

Immediately I went to the phone, and spoke to someone who said it would be alright for me to go in straight away. I really could not understand why I felt such an urge to go straight away, having just had quite a long drive, especially as my usual format was to go to bed almost immediately I arrived at Lotte's.

However, I did go straight away, and within minutes of arriving Margaret, who is a fellow Piscean and a natural chatterbox, was asking what I did, why I was travelling to her area etc.

I told her I was a medium, visiting the area to do services at the Portsmouth Church, and she seemed on the one hand shocked, but on the other relieved. Her actual words were "I'm sure you have been brought here for me". (We have laughed at this many times since that occasion, because she is not the type of person who believes she is so special that such an event could have been organised just for her). However, there were very serious reasons for her feeling that I would be able to help her. I told her I had one available sitting the following evening, and she said she would like to have it. It was probably one of the most remarkable sittings I've ever done from an evidential point of view, because it dealt with business matters in a very precise way, and in such a way that she was able to reorganise her life, something which was vital at the time.

After the sitting Margaret and I talked for a little while about the content of the sitting which was for me quite unusual dealing as it did with business in great depth. She then said she would like to come to the church demonstration on the Saturday night, and asked if Lotte and I would like to go back to her home for supper afterwards, which we happily accepted.

Margaret was, and still is, convinced that I was brought into her life to help her because five minutes before I telephoned to book the toning tables she had been desperately wondering where she could get help from.

In addition to this, one of the other ladies using the toning tables was walking very badly, so I asked her if she was all right. She told me she was in terrible pain because of spinal problems, and that she had developed a curvature at the bottom of the spine.

Unusually, I asked would she like some healing, and explained that I could guarantee nothing, but I would try to help her if she would like. She accepted, and lay down on one of the tables, and although she was a little tense, she did relax after a few minutes, and said she could feel something happening.

She then left, obviously sceptical, yet wanting to believe she could feel better.

The next day, when I saw Margaret, she said she had telephoned the lady to enquire if there was any change, and the pain she had for years had gone, but now she felt severe discomfort in both buttocks which felt like muscular pain. I subsequently gave her healing after supper on Saturday night, and then continued with absent healing — reports later were that she was feeling much better.

Margaret and I have become close personal friends, and began to meet socially whenever I visited the area. One day, over lunch, I told her the story of the young man who had survived the car accident, and how guilty I had always felt that I had not spoken to him, and her reply astounded me. Apparently her son's friend, the families knew each other and she, too, shared the sadness for the whole situation, remembering that on the day they heard of the tragedy she and her children had cried together.

I asked if she could send one of my little books of inspirational poetry to the family, in the hope that something therein could be of comfort to them, and this she duly did. Much later, I was able to meet the mother of the boy who had survived, and hope I was able to help and reassure her that help was at hand.

We should always remember that there are many of life's situations, which involve other people, which are not our business to judge. Sadly grief creates its own problems. I only know that where there is need for help the Spirit world point us in the right direction and then it is up to us to decide whether we want to help or not.

Margaret and I are still friends, and I feel we always will be. It is interesting to note that, having only known her for 15 months on the day my lovely friend Lotte passed to Spirit it was she I telephoned, to ask her to contact Ernie and help where she could, and it was at Margaret's home I stayed, when we went to Lotte's funeral. Margaret also helped to provide the refreshments after the funeral.

Do you really believe that we meet people coincidentally? I do not, as there are so many similar incidents that I believe those behind the scenes, our family and friends in Spirit, bring us together, for whatever vast experiences life will offer us.

I thank God each day of my life for the friendships I have made, and for the joy of knowing people like Lotte, Ernie and Margaret — my life would have certainly been much emptier without them.

KNOWLEDGE ABOLISHES FEAR

Some of you, upon reading this, may wonder why I don't simply tell the story, instead of analysing the communications, and the methods of communication. I do this partly to help ME to understand and partly to help you to believe that you may have gifts of communication, which you may have not yet developed. As yet, there is no fool-proof system by which we can receive and then give messages from the Spirit world, but during many years enough proof has been established that there is truth behind the theory that discarnate souls can communicate with those of us on earth. This ability knows no religious barriers, no barriers of colour or creed — they are only man-made excuses. Thank God we live in a somewhat enlightened age, where children, seeing and hearing Spirit people, are not always accused of telling lies, or simply using imagination.

When I was a little girl I frequently received smacks to my bottom for speaking the things that my mother was thinking — but I was just a little girl — and I wonder now why she did not investigate my abilities more closely, particularly now I know that my grandmother and great grandmother were both mediums, and that many members of my family regularly visited Spiritualist churches. I had never even heard of a Spiritualist church until the age of thirty three, when I first ventured into Fleetwood Church. I don't know if I feel cheated of knowledge or not. If I accept the belief that we are all in the right place at the right time, then I must accept that I was not meant to go into a Spiritualist church earlier than I did. Actually, I KNOW that had the knowledge of after life and my ability to communicate with that life come to my full attention any earlier I would have rejected it, for I had the responsibilities of bringing up a child, and I could not have neglected that responsibility, nor could I have shirked my duties as a wife, despite the unhappiness of my so-called marriage.

I refer to it in that way because I believe a marriage is a blending and bonding of two souls, something I have not yet experienced.

I lived a very unhappy and fearful existence for almost twenty years, and find myself smiling when other women tell me their life stories, and then say "You wouldn't understand." Mostly I do not bother to enlighten them, but I can say, in all honesty, that if mediums had not experienced sadness, trauma, loss and many other negative emotions, they would not have the storehouse of knowledge from which to draw to help and further the work they must do for the Spirit world.

This knowledge acts as a memory-bank and can enhance the quality of communications, for sometimes upon receiving information we FEEL rather than see what is being communicated, and if we had not had that understanding from where would that knowledge come? The answer is simple isn't it? Knowledge promotes knowledge instead of simply belief, and establishes a credibility between recipient and messenger, in this case a medium. Please query this, and test it if you wish, but never think that mediums and healers have no understanding of suffering or sadness, for to do so does them an incredible injustice.

However, remember also that as with any other profession there are varying degrees of standard of work, and it is for the discerning investigator to be exactly that — discerning.

I wish you well in your search for truth — remember to keep an open mind, an open heart, and leave the rest to spirit.

PROOF IS TRUTH IS PROOF

Another time which proved to me how well the Spirit world can work with us was when I was invited to give a lecture to members of the police force in Birmingham, the reason being to try to establish if mediums, and their evidence, could help the police in particular cases.

My good friend Mary, who sadly for me recently passed to Spirit, was happy to accompany me on this occasion, as it was in her area, and she knew exactly where I had to be. So we set off and arrived a little early, something I always try to do, in order to relax before commencing work.

We were escorted to a room in which to wait, and the officer who escorted us asked me if I was "game for a laugh". Being naturally curious I wanted to know why, and he said he wanted to play a joke on one of the officers who was attending the lecture. He further explained the content of the joke and asked if I could do anything with it. I made no promises but said I would see what I could do.

I really must explain at this point that I have NEVER, nor will I ever, use my work for Spirit in any way which would discredit the name of mediumship, not even for a joke.

We were then taken to the lecture room, where I was introduced, and the lecture proceeded, many of the men attending seeming rather embarrassed about my presence in their midst. I have since wondered if they thought I could read minds (many people seem to be under the impression that mediums read minds — I can assure you this is very far from the truth). We had a short break, followed by question time, and then a young officer closed the session by thanking me for the work I had done for them.

As I stood up to leave I suddenly remembered the conversation with the officer prior to entering the lecture room, and as the "victim" was sitting exactly opposite me it seemed the right time to say "I've been told there is someone here called John (name changed) and he knows something about (the situation I was told of)".

The poor man went as red as beetroot, and demanded to know who had told me! At this point my friend expected me to point in the direction of the policeman friend who had set him up, but something quite remarkable happened. A man from the Spirit world appeared directly in front of the policeman I had intended to tease and gave me reams of information, which I simply repeated, whereupon the poor man's face drained till he was as white as a sheet, his response being "Who told you all that? Nobody in this room knows about those things". I merely replied "Now, gentleman, you have something to think about. If that information could not have been given to me by anyone here where did I receive it from?". Mary and I left the room and were escorted to the senior officers' dining room, whilst the men attending went to the canteen to eat.

What had actually happened, of course, was that the father of the man I spoke to had actually chosen that very moment to make his presence known. He later let me know that his son really needed some help and guidance. It was at this point my "voice", as I call my Spirit helper, said I should offer to do the man a sitting.

I relayed this information to the officer in charge, who contacted the man in question and I did actually give him a sitting the contents of which were some of the most evidential I have ever received.

Please remember, always, that the content of any message is the choice and responsibility of the person communicating it — in this case the officer's father. When I started the sitting he very quickly re-established himself and seemed to want to give proof of up-to-date happenings, some of which his son did not know at that time, but which he verified within a matter of days.

A short time later he wrote to me to thank me for keeping him in my prayers, as well as family members who needed help at that time, and generally giving me an insight into what he had been doing since we had met.

He then wrote the following, which is largely self-explanatory — and I must say that I was very pleased he had acknowledged that I had conveyed these truths to him, because he had vehemently denied them during the sitting.

He wrote on 29th December 1990:
"Before I close I think you should know a couple of things about the conversation we had. When I arrived home that Friday I rang my mother in Scotland and told her of our meeting.

1: You said my mother had a weak right ankle. I said it was her wrist. My mother told me her right ANKLE was very weak and she kept "going over on it", but she had not told me in case I worried.

2: You said there was an old lady beside my father when he died, and that she was wearing an apron. I said he died alone. I was wrong. A farmer's wife — Old Mrs Wilson — was with my father when he died, and for the past 14 years I have not been aware of this.

3: You said my son was to see a doctor/consultant about his emotions. I said he wasn't. When I arrived home on that Friday, my wife told me that she had received a letter from a psychologist inviting Mark to take part in a survey/study regarding his emotions, and my wife had written back, stating we would be willing to assist.

Apart from those three things there were many other things you told me that were accurate. My colleagues at Birmingham were very interested in our conversation (refers of course to his sitting) when I returned on Monday. It was interesting to see their reactions when I told them what had been said. Even the sceptics were left bewildered."

This last portion of his letter thrilled me. So many people think that mediums are strange, spooky people, who merely offer

159

information without back-up evidence of the things they are saying, and here we have a rather more typical case of the way those in the Spirit world will, and have in the past so many times, taken God-given opportunities to prove themselves in the most evidential way possible. Consider for a moment how much thought must have gone into giving that particular police officer information that he would have to take away, and actually prove. And how clever of those in the Spirit world to know that this officer would happily go back to his colleagues and enthral and confuse them with knowledge of the real proofs he had received.

Doesn't this suggest that there really is an intelligence behind the communications we receive? Mediums can, as the magicians claim, provide certain generic information — those little tit-bits that can relate to absolutely everyone — but when the information is quite specific, what then of those worn-out theories?

Mediumship has stood the test of time, and will continue to do so, and no matter how often those who doubt, try to condemn us, we will continue to do that which we do best, and that is to allow the voice of Spirit to be heard by those who are genuinely seeking.

Just a final thought to those of you attending demonstrations of mediumship, where messages are being communicated through a medium. Sometimes people are a little too quick to judge the content of the messages, mistakenly believing those messages to be of little relevance, but unless you are the recipient of the message you cannot possibly judge, so please wait until you receive your own evidence before being too critical, and remember it is those people in the Spirit world who actually CHOOSE for themselves what information they wish us to have!

CHRISTMAS CHEER

CHRISTMAS EVE 1988

This time of the year brings so much emotion to the surface, particularly for those who have lost someone to the Spirit world. Christmas is, after all, a time when most people are thinking of getting together with friends and family, but the older we get we find that the family connections dwindle, and friendships change.

I have been very fortunate during the past 11 years, since I have been on my own, as friends have always invited me to their homes for Christmas. Ten years ago I stayed with my lovely friend and second mum Reta, in Market Rasen, a lady I have come to love and respect very much. We are not able to get together as much as I would like, but Reta is always there, quietly in the background of many people's lives.

We actually met at Stansted, during one of Don Galloway's seminars in 1986. Don's seminars were always booked up, and so my friend and I were very lucky to get places.

Previously I had always gone to Stansted for Blackpool week, and so this was to be a very different experience, and not knowing what to expect, I simply looked forward to it. I had, as usual taken far too many clothes, but in those days we always changed for evening, and had the shoes, bags, and jewellery all matching. And so, after the mammoth task of unpacking, I ventured downstairs. Most of the people were new to me, and it was a wonderful experience to meet so many people, all from different walks of life, all from different emotional and material backgrounds, gathering together to share time with the Spirit world. I remember walking around the grounds, enjoying the beauty of the day, visiting the tulip tree, which was, and still is to this day, a pilgrimage to so many people.

During this week I became acquainted with Gee Sumeray, who acted as hostess and secretary to Don. Gee was probably the most remarkable woman I had ever met, a true lady with a wonderful mind, generous Spirit, love in her heart for the underdog, and the mental energy to help everyone she came into contact with. I will remember my meeting with her forever. Not the usual gentle introduction one might expect from such a lady — oh no — she crooked her finger and beckoned, or rather summoned me to her presence, very gently but very firmly indeed. She told me she had heard a lot about me, and wanted to know more. She further informed me that I was to do her a private sitting, which I thought was rather cheeky, as I was a paying guest on the week, but I felt it would be the right thing to do, and anyway I could find no way of saying no to this lady.

We met at the appointed time, took the lift together, and she informed me that I was to undergo a test. (This did nothing at all for my already low self esteem, I can assure you). However, the sitting went ahead, and apparently all was well, for Gee said it was one of the best sittings she had had, and that she wanted me to do a sitting for a friend of hers. This turned out to be Reta — a lady I had had no real contact with. She seemed rather a private individual, and of course, I did not know any of these people at this stage, but am very glad I did come to know them very well indeed. Anyway, I did do Reta a sitting, and thought she was rather non-committal, and so thought I had probably not given her the evidence she really needed. It was at a much later date, when we had become firm friends, that Reta said that she could not respond too well because she was quite emotional due to the content of the sitting, during which I had, apparently, given her four pieces of proof that only her beloved husband, now in Spirit, could have provided.

CHRISTMAS MEMORIES

When I next saw Gee she told me how thrilled she was, and that she felt sure I would be working for Don Galloway the following year, and that is exactly what happened. I owe a lot to Gee, she was my friend, mentor, mum, supporter, as she was to so many people. I will write more about her later. For now I would like to concentrate on that meeting with Gee, leading to so much that was to become important to me. My contact with the Lynwood Fellowship, and with people like Reta. I realise how often I digress, but find it very difficult to simply keep on track. Anyway back to Christmas. My Christmas with Reta was to be one of many where the contacts with the Spirit world were very much a part of our times together. It would almost seem that once you are as involved with the Spirit world and its workings as I am, that nothing you do is separate from it, and how glad I am to know that. Now, that is not to say that whoever I stay with is in receipt of messages every five minutes. Actually it is the people who host me who receive less than anyone else, because wherever I stay I am allowed to be just "me", without any expectation of having to "sing for my supper", as I have heard other mediums report.

Mediumship is something, like any other vocation, that must have its time and place, and we must also know how to forget about work and simply "be". I am always happy to discuss the workings of the Spirit world, and the relevance of Spirit communications in our lives, but I do not give messages willy-nilly, because apart from anything else it is not sensible, and quite frankly can be quite boring to those listening. I learnt very long ago that it is far better to give one or two messages of quality, rather than a dozen bits and pieces of communication. The point of communication between the two worlds is to prove that discarnate souls, our loved ones, can and do communicate, and so there needs to be relevance to the messages, not just portions of messages.

Sometimes, in gentle ways, the loved ones of those people I am staying with, make their presence known. Often I am used without even knowing it is happening. One such event took place on one of my visits to Reta's lovely home. It was bedtime, and I was doing something in the kitchen whilst Reta tidied up the lounge. For no known reason I suddenly burst into song, which is dreadful as I cannot sing very well. The song was "Thanks for the memory". Those were the only words I sang to Reta that night, but they were enough to send her into a state of complete shock. It was the following day before she explained that that song had particular meaning to her, a connection with her Roy, and so we both believed he was with us that evening and simply wanted to let Reta know.

It is a long time since I have worked at Lynwood Fellowship but the memories of friendships formed will last forever.

DENMARK

MY DANISH FAMILY

I first visited Denmark about six years ago, having met some Danish women at Stansted Hall in England. Although I was attending a course there, I was asked to do some work, taking classes etc, as one of the mediums had not arrived. During the week, the Danish women introduced themselves to me, one of them telling me the most amazing story of how as a child she had gone to the Spirit world each night, having out of body experiences, and each night she was taught by some teacher in the Spirit world. She insisted that I was that teacher, which seemed a little weird, as I was not even born when this was happening to her. We enjoyed each other's company very much, during that first week, and at the end of the week I was invited to spend some time with one of the women. I thanked her and we made arrangements for the following year.

For the next three years or so I visited Denmark for private visits only. Then one day I was asked if I would be willing to do a public demonstration of clairvoyance at the Daniel Kirk, a Spiritualist Church in Copenhagen and the only one of its kind in Denmark. Of course I said I would be interested, and a meeting was set up for me to be introduced to the owner of the church, a man who is also a medium. I was to discover that this man had bought the church, a beautiful building which he had painted and decorated himself. There are regular church services, demonstrations and circles held there.

However, before working there, I was invited to meet him and his wife at their house on the outskirts of Copenhagen. We duly arrived, one Sunday afternoon, and it was then that I discovered that neither the man or his wife spoke English, and of course I speak no Danish. Thankfully, the woman I had met first in

England had perfect English, and so she acted as interpreter for us all.

We had coffee and cake, a great Danish tradition, and then I was asked by the man if I would like to have some brandy. I declined as I do not particularly like drinking, especially when I am unsure of my environment, which I certainly was, if only because of not understanding the language.

During the next hour I was asked many more times if I would like some brandy, being told that it was a very fine brandy. So eventually I agreed just to please them.

I was served some neat brandy, and thankfully I still had some coffee, so I sipped the brandy and drank coffee immediately afterwards, until eventually all the brandy was gone. The man's wife then asked if I would give them messages, to which I replied, quite indignantly "Certainly not. I never open up to Spirit when I have had alcohol". For reasons not understood by me everyone visibly relaxed, a lot of Danish was spoken and quite suddenly we left. Immediately we got outside the woman I was staying with said "Well, you passed the test". By this time I was very confused, and also a little curious, so I asked her to explain exactly what she meant. She laughed, and told me that the "test" was to find out if I would be willing to work with Spirit after having alcohol. Apparently, they had had some bad experiences of mediums who preferred their "spirits" from a bottle!

Shortly after that experience I was booked for the church, and so I looked forward to seeing it and working there — not knowing quite what to expect, but taking it as yet another challenge organised by the Spirit world.

The day of my first public demonstration in Denmark was something of a nightmare, as I have always found that "firsts" are. I was incredibly nervous and restless (which I now know is the Spirit workers' way of letting me know they are blending their energy with mine throughout the day of a demonstration), and prayed constantly to Spirit, hoping that I would not let them down.

We arrived at the church and were met by the owners who took us down some stairs where there was a very large room with tables and chairs. Here I was to wait until the time of the demonstration.

It was at this time, also, that I was to meet for the first time Wenche and Bjarne, who are now a part of my Spiritual family, and with whom I stay when I visit Denmark.

My interpreter for that first visit was a lady from Sweden who I met once and never saw again. For the second visit my interpreter was Wenche, and I remember being rather irritated by her, as she seemed quite shy and awkward. I realise now that my lack of experience of working in a foreign country very much affected my mood, and I have apologised for my behaviour since that first time.

After the first visit Wenche sometimes interpreted, and sometimes a man worked with me, and little by little Wenche and I came to understand and respect each other, for our mutual love of the Spirit world, and for our joint need to get things absolutely right for them.

After going to Denmark for some seven years my contact with my original hostess was broken, and for about 18 months I didn't go. It was, therefore, something of a surprise to be contacted by Wenche one day, and asked if I would go to Denmark to work for a Union which she had started with her husband. I did not immediately feel thrilled at the thought of going there — feelings I could not fully explain — but I did after a couple of requests agree to go, and how very happy I am that I changed my mind.

On the day of my journey I was full of misgivings, for reasons I choose not to go into, but here I was again, going to a Foreign country, to stay at the house of people I did not know very well. I had received from Wenche a programme of events which would occur during my visit, and she told me that she and her husband would meet me at the airport, so I took a deep breath and got on with it!

When I arrived at Copenhagen airport I was relieved to recognise Wenche. The first hurdle was over, and we went directly to the house in Olstykke. What a lovely surprise that was — I had always stayed in Copenhagen and I simply had no idea how beautiful the countryside was, and such a short distance from the city — only half an hour by car.

There was, however, no time to investigate further, for we were due to be on the Island of Fyn that evening for the first demonstration, and so after quickly unpacking and finding clean clothes, make-up, etc, we got back into the car and took an hour long drive to the ferry, followed by a ferry trip, then another long drive the other side, the journey taking us almost four hours in total. During the trip I spent a lot of time telling Wenche and Bjarne about my disappointments with the British media, because every time they show programmes about mediums they seem to show us in a poor light. Imagine then my horror when we arrived and were told that a TV crew was on its way to film the evening's events. Of course, I expressed my feelings, and said that I would not be willing for the demonstration to be filmed by TV people.

There was a discussion by the organiser from Fyn, Wenche and Bjarne, after which they then asked me if I would reconsider, as it would help them to establish greater credibility in Denmark, on behalf of Spirit. It was at this point that the TV people arrived, and we discussed for half an hour the right approach until finally I told them I would agree. They then said they could film for 15 minutes only, then they must leave. I was furious to think that they expected me to conduct a partial service for Spirit, allow them to disrupt it, and I was supposed to pick up the threads.

The important thing before any demonstration is preparation, and I was very concerned that disruption could be detrimental to the loving communications I usually established.

However, after further discussion I suggested that the first 20 people to come in would be the people I would do a demonstration for - I further suggested that the TV crew could then leave, then the rest of the people who had arrived could come into the room and we could continue with our evening for Spirit.

This we did, having a wonderful evening where the evidence flowed freely. We later saw a video recording of the news report which appeared later that evening - a very fair report offering the evenings events exactly as they occurred.

The most joyful part to me was that during the short newscast the two people who had received communication offered their analysis of the evidence they had been offered, both confirming what they had been told was correct. The final comment from the reporter was that for the first time in Denmark it had been proven there was life after death. What joy, and what a relief to know that there are journalists who are willing to be objective.

MY DANISH FAMILY HERE

I am constantly amazed at how much real evidence can be received and given in a country where I do not understand the language. During a demonstration on a bleak, snowy, Tuesday night, this was proven yet again when a communicator from Spirit spoke of having been shot in the head. I saw a scene which included a single orange painted house, behind which there was a large forest. Unfortunately no one accepted the contact, until I further added receiving the names of Karl and Johan. At this a woman gasped and she said she knew Karl-Johan! Apparently this young man had gone into a forest with a gun and shot himself. At the very edge of the forest there was a solitary orange painted house, just as described. Further substantive evidence of survival was given to several people who included a reporter from the Danish BT Newspaper. Naturally the newspaper reported the dramatic evening's evidence which in turn has resulted in me accepting further invitations for the future.

TELEPHONE TO THE DEAD

During one of my visits to Denmark, courtesy of the Star of Hope, I was asked if I would be willing to have a reporter sit in the demonstration, which was to take part in Gentoffte Library, Copenhagen, and would I allow myself to be interviewed afterwards? As I could see no reason why this would not be alright I agreed. On arriving at the library with Wenche and Bjarne we saw it filling up very quickly, as it had done in the past when I had demonstrated there.

There was no mention of the reporter, but I noticed a man who came to sit on my left, an elderly man who was fiddling with a note book and pen.

I was introduced by Wenche in Danish, and then when it was my turn to work I began, as usual, by saying a little prayer (my way of inviting the Spirit people to work with us). During the prayer the man muttered something, which was a little off-putting, then when I did the introductory talk he interrupted me again, and finally when I began the clairvoyance. By this time I had had enough, and asked that "something be done". The organiser asked the man to leave, my reaction being "Oh dear, that was the reporter and now I have failed to please the organisers because they wanted his publicity". However, knowing always that my job is to promote Spirit in the best way possible I ploughed on, and was very relieved at the end of the demonstration to be introduced to two young men, one of whom was the reporter for a newspaper called BT and the other his photographer. Below is an extract from a report written by Nikolas Buchardt in the Danish national newspaper BT from 20th April 1997.

(TRANSLATED FROM DANISH)

TELEPHONE TO THE DEAD

The dead queued up to talk to the living, when the English medium Val Williams demonstrated at the Library, in Hellerup. If you believe in these things, the evening proved that Spirit is both very keen on making contact and very humorous.

Is it her, whispered someone in the row behind me , when a little English lady entered the hall at Heilerup library -

Others must have shared her surprise, with her cropped hair with highlights, the green suit and outsized glasses, the medium looks more like one of the spectators to the evenings' demonstration than the leading star, who is said to be able to contact the dead and pass on messages from the other side.

But it IS her the 200 people have waited for while the caretaker was busy bringing extra chairs into the very unspiritual looking hall, in order to make room for everyone.

When the mixed audience of double breasted suits and the more alternative look is seated the organiser from ¹¹Between Heaven and Earth" bids everyone welcome and gives out notices of next month's programme.

The organizer asked the audience to quieten down so that the "energies can build up" This is the signal for the Clairvoyant Englishwoman to begin. "I will start with a prayer so we can build a good energy and a feeling of love up. I ask you all to think of your Spirit friends and family, who I know live on as spirit people, and by a shared feeling of love and trust we will tonight contact our loved ones, who have passed on" begins Val Williams.

While Val Williams, with her eyes shut, prays for the evening she asks the spirits, who in her opinion are waiting to make contact with the living, to come forward and speak to her.

THE SPIRITS HAVE WAITED

"The Spirits will often speak about the past to prove who they are, the person you knew and that they are still alive. Many have waited for months, or years even up to 50 years to make contact, so if you recognize anything I say, speak up loud and clear, so they can get a chance to speak to you."

"Is there someone wearing a watch which belonged to a male family member" -A woman at the front answers at once that her watch used to belong to her late father. "I feel that your father had something pressing on his chest - can you understand this? The woman answers that her father died of a heart-attack. Val Williams then says that someone else is with him "it is a young man who was kept artificially alive for some time" A woman at the back of the hall answers that it could be her brother who was kept on a respirator. The English medium then explains that the family had many difficulties in deciding to turn the respirator off. The woman confirms this. Val Williams then describes the brothers' looks and personality while alive "you often feel something tickling your neck" says the medium, to which the woman laughingly answers "Yes" That is your brothers way of telling you he is there - he also says you are to watch for the 26th June, or the days around that date.

Val Williams contact with the Spirit, who appear to address her from the right, often starts with some general questions addressed to the people in general "Is there someone here who knew a young man who drowned? Is there someone called Peter? Is there someone here with creative abilities? Is there anyone whose brother committed suicide?" Most descriptions are picked up by one or more of the people, some are blatantly trying to make the information fit themselves and the people they have known. HOWEVER Val Williams often dismisses them whilst she searches for someone else who has not yet spoken up. Once she finds t finds the right person , the description of the Spirit becomes precise and it

is rare for people to refute the messages and personalities who make contact via Val Williams, in the increasingly oxygen starved room.

DAD ARE YOU THERE?

"Is there a Christina amongst us?" A young woman answers "Yes," After the woman also answers Yes to a connection with Sweden, the medium confirms that the man sitting next to the young woman is her father and that their mother/wife is in Spirit. "Your wife tells me you never would listen to her while she was alive, but now you are always asking her advice - is that right?" the medium asks the man. He blushes and admits that is so. It feels as if the death was recent, and Val Williams then describes the circumstances "Your wife had her hair done just before she died and she was very dissatisfied with the result," Father and daughter laugh at the memory and Val Williams description of her vanity and humour were accepted. "You combed her hair after she died" she said to the man "and I have to tell you that you did it all wrong." The man and his daughter are laughing, while he says with surprise "But I thought it was nice. Forget it, she is very dissatisfied with it. I am also told that you have started to iron your own clothes." The man explains that he has only now started ironing his own clothes since his wife's death. "Your wife says that you iron your clothes so badly in order to get other people to do it for you," continues the medium, while the entire congregation is howling with laughter and the man is forced to admit he would rather have other people do his clothe, The last part of the message is for the daughter who is asked if she knows anyone who is going to South Africa.

CARNATION ON GLASS TABLE

The daughter answers that some friends are going to South Africa. Val Williams explains that this message from the mother is proof that she still exists in another place. "I am also getting a picture of a carnation cut off near the head and placed on a glass table. Keep an eye open for that as it will be from her " says the English woman. Shortly after that she explains that her energy is gone and she is unable to continue.

One and a half hours have passed with descriptions of illness, deaths, persons and small everyday details, The congregation slowly leaves the hall. The 15/16 who had a message are clearly touched by the words describing their dead loved ones lives.

Val Williams looks like any housewife, very tired, as she disconnects the microphone and heads off for a late dinner.

THE INTERVIEW - SHE SEES THAT WHICH WE DON'T SEE

Val Williams explains "For me contact with the Spirit world is quite natural. I was born with these abilities and do not consider it peculiar in anyway. Val Williams is Clairvoyant, which, using the English mediums own words means an ability to see things clearly. "As a child I had a friend no one else could see. she was a natural part of my life. My mother always laid an extra place setting for her at meal times. If we caught the bus I would yell if anyone sat down beside me because they were sitting on my friend." explains Val Williams, who travels the world in order to share that world with us in the more material world.

It was not until the early 80's she began to understand what she describes as her gift " I had lived with it all my life, but you need maturity to be able to understand it-it was not until then I realized my gift could be used to help people and for Spirit to communicate. That is why I began demonstrating in public," says Val Williams.

She is able to switch her contact with the Spirit world on and off, very much like an electric light switch - It would be impossible to live with constant contact of the things she can see.

THE CONNECTION

"When I am in a group of people as I am now, an imagined door next to me opens up . This is where the spirit people come and talk to me. It is a bit like a telephone connection with someone abroad. There is a kind of delay of a few seconds sometimes, and Spirit always speak English to me, which is very practical. Danish is a very difficult language, so if I am asked to give a name or place name. I have problems."

Val Williams can't predict the future. She is the link between our world, and the Spirit world, facilitating contact between those who want to make contact. But she has other abilities, which uses in her personal consultations.

"I am a healer and I see auras, and can tell if there is anything wrong with a person, explains Val Williams."

According to Val the Spirits are only interested in proving they continue to exist, and are happy. That is why a lot of time is spent on small details that people can recognize. Whether this is evidence can only the person receiving the message judge.

This journalist can only say that her diagnosis of my left knee was right!

Footnote

During the course of the interview I had mentioned that the young man had obviously some problem with his knee, possibly due to an accident at an earlier time - this because my helper briefly linked me to his knee in a healing way.

During the next visit the reporter came for a private sitting and brought someone else, who very much needed evidence of life after death - a testimonial in itself I believe that the power of the Spirit can prove itself whenever there is a genuine need, and to those who are sincerely seeking.

The Spirit communicators obviously need ,sometimes, a little publicity of their truth - that there is no death - if only to remind us all that we cannot merely concentrate on our own needs and wishes. Our thoughts need to be more forward looking. How wonderful that we are able to provide, through the communications from our loved ones, help, and loving guidance to all who need help, and thank God for those, such as this young reporter who offered to the reading public such an unbiased and honest report.

(P.S. Since this time I have bought some smaller spectacles!)

HOW HAS LIFE REALLY SHAPED ME?

For any child who has the KNOWING, life can be quite complicated. Do you have a child, or grandchild, who seems always to want to assert their own thinking rather than listen to you and, if so, do you feel threatened by their need to be an individual?

I well remember the number of occasions when I "let out" some secret that my mother had, because of my inside knowing. Just thoughts at the time, but those thoughts have now become the voices I hear, and I sometimes think that if I had had the voices when I was much younger I would have had less insecurities, and less smacks, because I would have been able to know what I knew, instead of always testing the system.

Watching TV quiz games was no fun for the people watching with me, because I would blurt out the answers, even though I had no knowledge of the subject. People would start conversations and I would finish them for them, again without thinking my way into the situation, but with the words coming straight out of my mouth without my knowing WHY.

WHY became my favourite word — oh now I see, I have struck a chord in you somewhere — so you know such a child do you? Isn't it strange that with the children who question the most, there is always another question to follow the answer they are given?

Almost in a state of rebellion, because no-one seemed to like me being right, I began NOT to wish to communicate my seemingly strange thoughts, which I now feel was a great pity. Had I been brought up in the family of, say, Spiritualists, I would have been encouraged to understand my "gifts" from a very early age, instead of believing that the thoughts, voices and visions were more of a curse. Such ignorance still abounds today, with children having the knowing and parents and grandparents fearing it.

"You'll end up in a mental home" is just one of the silly things adults say to children who are a little "different". What a terrible thing to say — how much better for the grown ups to be exactly that — grown up about the situation, and with an adult attitude approaching the child in a gently probing and questioning way. There is nothing worse for a child than to be considered untruthful, and I can assure you the Spirit people would never offer information to a child which would cause them harm, mentally or emotionally.

Looking back over my life now I realise that the Spirit communicators treated me very gently indeed, never intruding into my life, never forcing information upon me, but choosing exactly the right moment for me to come to investigate properly their intent towards me.

I did not have a very good relationship with my parents, my father working away most of the time, and he and my mother never seeming to get on very well, and so as a child I felt quite isolated many times, especially as by the age of four and a half I had a new sister for my mother to take care of.

When I was thirty three I began attending the local Spiritualist church, and from having contact with like-minded people I began to establish a pattern of receiving inspirational poetry, something I had no talent for whatsoever, and so I began to question again WHY, why me, where was it coming from, what was the purpose of it? It became so much a part of me that I found, for a little time, that I couldn't shut off the stream of inspirational thought.

These "thoughts" have been put together, some of them in a little booklet entitled "Somebody loves you". When I read them I feel very humbled for I know that I, Val Williams, could not have written them, and so again I asked questions. I sometimes wonder why they persevered with me as I questioned so very much, but I am sure that is why they know I trust them because we have, during a long period of time, established an understanding that is almost business-like, a two way respect.

Whilst I came to respect, very much, those who came to inspire me, I also realised that if I was like an open channel, not understanding what was happening, I would not be able to function adequately on a day to day basis with the "normal" tasks of life, such as caring for a family, looking after a home, working, and being a group leader for the junior sea cadets, all of which I was coping with at the time.

I somehow knew, without anyone telling me (that arrogance again I used to think) that I must establish a means of allowing myself to be used as a receiver of information, at times that suited me, in order that I could not be accused of neglecting my daily tasks.

The best way seemed to be that I should establish the thought that I would sit for half an hour each evening, with pen and paper, in order that the Spirit inspirers could bring their words of wisdom to me. At this stage I had no idea of WHY they would want to, or what future purpose there could be, but I was willing to be used as an instrument by higher minds.

This established, for about a six year period, a regular pattern of thought transference from the Spirit inspirers to me, all of which I wrote down, sometimes pushing it to the back of a drawer afterwards, and sometimes reading it the following day. I now know that they were testing how much of their inspiration I would be willing to write down exactly as I received it, without changing it, or colouring it with my own thoughts, but at the time I merely wrote everything down without questioning too much.

During those years it became increasingly obvious that my marriage was nothing more than a sham. Through many public messages I was encouraged to know that my Spirit loved ones, my grandmother, aunts, and a variety of friends, knew of the restrictions and the sadness in my life, and that they were offering their supportive love to me.

My marriage ended in December 1987, in ways that I could not have envisaged, but for which I will always be grateful to the Spirit people who had helped me through every day of the previous 19 years — without their loving encouragement that "one day" things would change I could not have carried on.

When that "one day" had come and gone I, the Val Williams I now am, came to understand fully how the Spirit world had been her guidance, her comfort and her strength, and I vowed then that I would always be willing to be a channel for their peace, their love, and their understanding, in gratitude for my life.

Life really began for me then. Strange to look back now, many years later. I sometimes wonder WHO that person was, that other Val Williams. Knowledge, true knowledge is a wonderful thing, and only when we establish a pattern of KNOWING and trusting that knowing do we truly free ourselves to be the person we were always meant to be. I look back now and wonder how I, the I who is now confidently working with the Spirit world, with the courage to say to all who wish to hear it "I talk with voices from the so-called dead you know", survived all the lost years. The times when I knew that somewhere I should be able to find a greater truth than I was currently experiencing, and a blending with other people who thought and felt as I do, and I cannot imagine that I would ever refuse to take the time to listen to someone who is struggling to establish their personal truth.

You and I are still children you know, for each day of our lives there is something to learn, hurdles to overcome, new truths to establish, and many times we reach out to other people to help us, to give us some understanding and we find ourselves disappointed. WHY do that, when there is a source of knowledge that is close to you that can help you better than any other living person possibly can? Establish for yourself your link with your own soul, through quiet times, through meditation perhaps, and learn that the voices within and the thoughts that won't go away, are the guidance you need.

Feeling the fear of change and new ideals is not the problem, the problem is when you don't have the courage to follow through. As a medium I may be privileged to give you signposts, or hints, or comfort when you have need, but I cannot establish for you a KNOWING — for that comes from your own soul, your heart and your mind. Let your logical mind confirm for you that which your soul wants you to know and have the courage to follow it through, and like the child who dares to stride out in life, knowing that you are watching from a safe distance, know that your life is guided by unseen friends, and therefore your world is safe.

Having skipped quite quickly through my life, giving you an outline of the way in which the Spirit world established their ability to communicate with me, I feel sure you will be interested in the story of a two and a half year old little girl who had the most amazing link with the Spirit world.

In 1988, having been away from the area for a couple of weeks, working for Spirit, I was having a rare night off. I was at this time living at my mother's, waiting for the divorce proceedings to go ahead, when I had a sudden urge to go to the Open Circle at Fleetwood Church, so rushed down there, arriving a few minutes prior to the start of the service.

A young man came straight over to me, asking if I was Val Williams. He had never seen me, but had been told about me, and he felt I could help him. We spoke later, when he began to tell me the story of his little girl, then two and a half years of age who, each night at about midnight, got out of bed, got dressed and prepared to go out to meet someone. That someone turned out be to be the young man's grandfather, who was in the Spirit world, and as he was telling me the story the gentleman linked in with me to tell me his version of the story. He told me who he was, and further said that in the house the young man was visiting there was a wardrobe, and that the little girl was having to be removed from the wardrobe. He then went on to say that there was a back gate with a broken lock, which was not suitable and must be fixed, and then he said he was worried because the little girl, being curious, may electrocute herself if a faulty plug was not dealt with.

The young man was staying temporarily at his grandfather's house, having recently moved back from the Isle of Man with his young wife and the little girl. I asked the gentleman in Spirit why he had come and he told me he was very worried about his daughter, who was the aunt of the young man — apparently she had some health problems. He went on to say that there would be no problems with the little girl, as he had been able to get across his concern for his daughter, this being his reason for needing to communicate with someone who could help her.

Of course I told the young man everything his grandfather had said, and away he went.

He telephoned me the next day to say his daughter had slept through the night for the first time since they had arrived, that he had fixed the bolt on the back gate, found and sorted out the electric plug, and that the baby-sitter had to remove the little girl three times from the wardrobe whilst she was baby-sitting, so that he and his wife could attend the Spiritualist Church.

He then asked if I would like to call round for a cup of coffee, and I said I would be delighted, on condition that I could meet the child, and know for myself that everything was alright. We arranged for me to call at 9.30 that evening.

When I arrived there was a lot of tension in the house, tension from the young man, his wife and another young couple. The father of the child suddenly said to the little girl in very agitated tones "Well, go on, tell her, tell the lady what you see". Aware of the tension I asked that all the adults not to transfer their fears to the child, who was quite happy.

I then asked her about the grandfather, and she looked a little distressed and pointed to her hand. Thankfully, the grandfather linked in to me and told me he had burnt his hand when on board a fishing boat, so I asked her if he was alright now, and she suddenly looked up at me, smiled and skipped to the other side of the room, very happily.

I left shortly afterwards, thinking that would be the last I would see of them and thanking God that I had been allowed to deal with the situation, as the grown-ups were thinking of having the child exorcised, thereby transferring all their fears to her, and possibly causing her a great deal of distress.

Some ten years later, again on impulse, I decided to go to visit a friend in Blackpool, and realising that she would be at a psychic group she ran I knew I would have to go there if I wanted to see her. I had been there some ten minutes when a man approached me and said "You are Val Williams aren't you — you won't remember me, but you came to our house ten years ago and helped my daughter". I said "Of course I remembered, I would never forget her." He then pointed to the other side of the room, and told me that the young lady he was pointing to was that very girl, and that since my visit, he and his wife had made it their business to investigate the truths of Spirit return, in order that they could help their daughter to develop her Spiritual gifts in the most natural way, with no fears whatsoever.

What a privilege, and how happy I felt to know that I had been used to establish for someone else a knowledge and a confidence it had taken me so many years to find.

Maybe one day I will, on impulse, turn up at a demonstration of mediumship to discover that the demonstrator is a grown up version of the little girl I met so many years previously, and who was now working for the cause of the Spirit world in the most positive and loving way, offering a truth to those enquiring, helping others to find their individual truth, and giving comfort and reassurance where needed.

THE VOICE THAT GUIDES

How many times have you said "I've got a hunch" or "I've a strong feeling" or "A little voice in my head said..."?

Do you realise there are many times that these thoughts and feelings can be translated into something very real and tangible, if you investigate properly?

You may have already said "Oh no, it was just a thought, a hunch", and if that is your choice fine, but I am finding more and more people are wanting to understand what guides them, what their intuition really is, and how they can best use this knowledge in their daily lives. Sometimes to give them more confidence in their own abilities and knowledge, and sometimes to help them to deal with other people, or help other people.

Whilst we are individuals we are none of us islands, our lives are intertwined more ways than we often realise, and sometimes our paths cross although we don't know why, but after a time we realise that it is because we are on some new path of learning.

Some fifteen years ago I began consciously trying to find out more about the voice that guides me. I have heard him so many times — a beautifully modified male voice, which seems to resonate inside me (earlier in the book I have referred to him as the voice of my soul — he is not some part of me, but a totally separate personality), and does so in such a positively clear way that, having tested him, I can never doubt that he has my best interests at heart or that he knows what he is saying.

My voices began when I was a child, when I heard inside my head the voice of a little girl, a different voice from my own, and which later progressed via thoughts, and with a lot of self discipline until I knew if the voices were male, or female, whether they were young or old, and from intense periods of questioning and

185

understanding the responses, I have built a dossier of knowledge that has taken me away from the realms of belief into a knowledge. No-one can take away from another person their knowledge (though many may try).

Now I know many of you will say "But what about the schizophrenic — doesn't he hear voices in his head?". Of course, it has been established that some people with mental disorders do hear voices, but what we are talking about here are not voices that cause harm or offer random information, but rather the voices of my loved ones and yours, offering help, guidance, proof of their presence in our lives and a means of finding comfort through the truths they establish with and for us.

I cannot expect everyone reading this to know or even believe what I say is true, but I hope you will challenge and investigate your own hunches or feelings a little more.

I have had the great privilege of speaking to a group of police officers, to psychologists, psychiatrists, doctors etc, all people who must follow their so called hunches if they are to be successful, and many interesting conversations have taken place between us when we throw back and forth ideas about where hunches come from, and why we suddenly "know" that something is true. It is that knowing that you need to investigate, for that is the knowledge that resides in you, often put there by the voices that guide you, as they guide me.

Of course it would have been foolish to simply believe everything my voices have told me, and to follow their guidance or instruction, and so I have always questioned and asked for proof that their guidance was to be for the best, and each and every time they have proven themselves to me, so that I no longer doubt.

In the early days of investigating my knowledge, I did so with a great deal of enthusiasm, which has resulted in me sometimes being called the 'enthusiastic medium' by some people who attend my seminars and classes. This is a title I am proud to have for the word enthusiastic has movement to it — it feels strong and good, and I hope I will always have some of the joy and enthusiasm I have always had, to continue to allow my voices to guide me to help others.

There are some things which just cannot be imagined, but when I look back over the last 20 years I am amazed that someone who always doubted herself so very much could today say with assurance to audiences coming to see her demonstrations of mediumship "I am right and I know it, and I can prove it!". Sounds a little arrogant doesn't it? Maybe some people are afraid of others' knowledge and therefore find it easier to claim they are ignorant. My knowing should not make you feel inferior or doubtful, but rather it should enthuse you with the knowledge that if I can have such confidence in my knowing then so can you, by systematically investigating the thoughts that move you!

Why don't you give it a try?

The next time you feel your thoughts are directing you in a certain way, why not try to find out why and how your thoughts are motivating you, and in time you too may establish contact with something that is more than a thought.